8 New York NYSTP Grade 5 Math Practice Tests

A eight-step adventure for New York Grade 5 thinkers

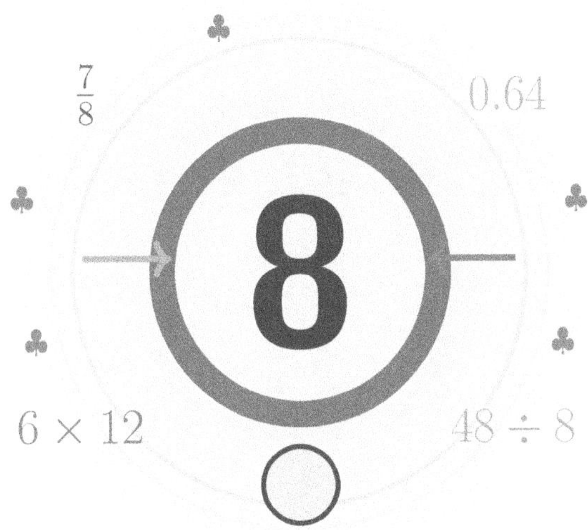

Eight full tests, a focused quick review, and helpful support that turns Grade 5 practice in The Empire State into steady, confident growth from page one to the final check.

Jay Daie and Reza Nazari

Copyright ©

Testinar Inc

Published by Testinar Inc

Testinar.com

New York Mathematicians, Lace Up

A eight-step trail built for steady, brave thinking

An Invitation to Grade 5 in New York

This practice book is your steady companion for eight tests, not a place to be perfect. Math is a lot like a New York skyline – it grows tall because every floor was framed with care.

Use these eight tests like stepping-stones. Take one test at a time, check your answers honestly, and notice which skills need more attention. Small improvements add up across seven rounds.

Watch

Watch what the problem actually wants from you.

Choose

Choose the operation, model, or table that fits.

Polish

Check labels, units, and the final word of the question.

A strong habit for New York mathematicians: read carefully, estimate when it helps, show your steps, and keep going even when a question feels tricky. That is how steady math confidence is built.

A Simple Path Through Eight Tests

A simple routine that turns practice into progress

Step 1: Open

Open the warm-up review and use it.

Spend a few minutes waking up your memory before the test begins.

Step 2: Test

Take the test with steady focus.

Work in a calm spot and focus on careful thinking before speed.

Step 3: Reflect

Notice what was sharp and what was shaky.

Circle missed questions and notice which topics keep showing up.

Step 4: Sharpen

Practice the shaky skills before the next round.

Read the explanation, repair the work, and bring that lesson into the next test.

A Good 8-Week New York Rhythm

Week 1	Take Test 1 and frame your first floor.
Week 2	Take Test 2 and slow down on word problems.
Week 3	Take Test 3 and lift fraction and decimal work.
Week 4	Take Test 4 and pay close attention to labels and units.
Week 5	Take Test 5 and compare your habits with your first test.
Week 6	Take Test 6 and practice staying calm during tricky questions.
Week 7	Take Test 7 and crown your tower with calm, careful work.
Week 8	Take Test 8 and finish the journey with calm, careful, confident work.

About These Eight Tests

What these eight practice tests help students build

These three practice tests prepare Grade 5 students in the Empire State for the New York NYSTP with the steady focus of a builder reading blueprints. The goal is bigger than only getting answers right. Students are practicing how to read closely, choose a strategy, solve carefully, and explain their work when needed.

Selected-Response Questions

Students solve the problem and choose the best answer. Estimating first and crossing out weak choices can save time and points.

Constructed-Response Questions

Students show their thinking, steps, models, or explanations. Even when unsure, writing what they know can help organize the problem.

Grade 5 Skills You Will Practice Often

- place value, comparing numbers, and rounding
- multi-digit addition, subtraction, multiplication, and division
- fractions, decimals, and mixed numbers
- perimeter, area, volume, and measurement conversions
- coordinate points, patterns, graphs, and tables
- geometry and multi-step word problems

What strong work looks like on the NYSTP: the answer is correct, the steps are clear, the labels or units are included, and the final result makes sense.

Move Smart, Think Calm

Smart moves for calm, careful problem solving

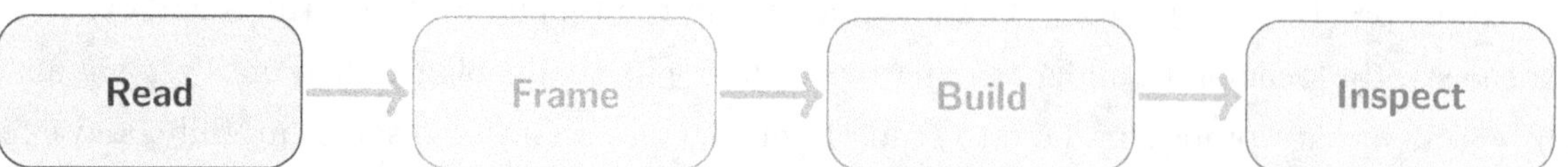

Pre-Flight

- pencil sharp, paper smooth
- read directions completely
- decide to be careful first

Flight

- underline what is asked
- estimate when helpful
- show your steps cleanly

Turbulence

- cross out impossible choices
- switch to a model or sketch
- skip, breathe, return

Landing

- check labels and units
- reread the question one last time
- be sure the answer fits

A calm reset for the NYSTP: When the test gets loud, work like a quiet morning at the top of a skyscraper – still, sharp, and high above the noise.

The Confident Mathematician

Confidence grows when New York students practice, reflect, and keep going

Trade the Panic Voice for a Coach Voice

Instead of thinking...	Try telling yourself...
This is too tricky.	Tricky problems train my brain.
I do not get it.	I can break it down or draw it out.
Why even try?	Each try makes the next try easier.
I always blank out.	I can take a slow breath and start with what I know.

Confidence Builders

- track scores and small wins
- notice one thing that improved today
- fix mistakes instead of hiding from them

A The Empire State Truth

A bluebird does not need a big stage. It picks the next branch and sings.

A powerful promise for this book: I will slow down, show my work, learn from corrections, and let practice make me stronger across all eight tests.

Eight-Test Growth Log

A simple way to notice growth across all eight New York tests

How to Use This Page

After each test, write your score, one topic that felt strong, and one next step. Each test is a new floor in your tower. Notice how high you can already see.

Test	Score	Highlight	Repair Goal
Test 1			
Test 2			
Test 3			
Test 4			
Test 5			
Test 6			
Test 7			
Test 8			

A smart reflection question: Did my score change because I knew more math, checked my work better, or stayed calmer? Sometimes the answer is all three.

Ready, Steady, Solve

Fast habits that warm up your brain before the real problem solving begins

Before the First Question

- read the directions all the way through
- look over the page without rushing
- begin with a clear pencil and an even clearer plan

While You Work

- underline what the problem really wants
- estimate when it helps you spot mistakes
- keep your work organized enough to easily check

Before You Turn It In

- check labels, units, and decimal points
- reread your final answer one more time
- make sure the answer truly fits the question

If Pressure Shows Up

- pause and take one slow breath
- solve only the next smallest part
- remember that one hard problem does not decide the whole test

A New York truth for the NYSTP: being ready does not mean feeling perfect. It means feeling prepared enough to think clearly and to keep going.

Big Ideas, Quick Map

A simple map of the big Grade 5 math ideas tested on the NYSTP

Why This Page Helps

Grade 5 math feels much easier to review when New York students know which skill family a question belongs to. Once they can name the family, they can focus practice in the right place instead of guessing what to study next.

Number Sense

Place value, decimals, fractions, and comparison

Operations

Multi-step computation, patterns, and reasoning

Measurement and Geometry

Area, volume, graphs, shapes, and coordinates

A useful review move: when you miss a question, do not stop at "wrong." Ask which skill family it came from. That single question points you straight toward the smartest next round of practice.

Grade 5 Skill Snapshot

Big domains and the kind of work students are expected to do

Domain	Focus Skills
Operations and Algebraic Thinking	Describe numerical patterns, compare how terms change, and reason about relationships in a rule or sequence.
Number and Operations in Base Ten	Use place value understanding and perform operations with whole numbers and decimals.
Number and Operations with Fractions	Compare fractions, find equivalent fractions, add and subtract fractions with like denominators, and multiply a fraction by a whole number.
Measurement and Data	Convert units, interpret line plots, and solve problems involving perimeter, area, and volume.
Geometry	Plot points on the coordinate plane and classify two-dimensional figures by their properties.

Study tip: if one domain feels shaky, spend extra time there before the next test instead of trying to review everything at once.

How Parents Can Help

Support for New York families that feels calm, useful, and realistic

What This Book Is Designed to Do

This book gives Grade 5 students eight opportunities to practice New York math in a real test-style setting and then learn from what happened. Empire practice is short and consistent: a small habit grows a tall skyline. The biggest gains usually come from short routines, honest review, and encouragement that feels steady rather than stressful.

What Is the NYSTP?

NYSTP stands for **N**ew **Y**ork **S**tate **T**esting **P**rogram. It is given to Grade 5 students across New York to measure progress on important math standards.

What Helps Most

- praise effort, patience, and clear work
- keep sessions short, regular, and predictable
- ask what your child learned from a mistake
- review missed problems without blame

What Gets in the Way

- turning practice into punishment
- rushing through hard problems just to finish
- comparing one child's score to another's
- focusing only on the final number

Sharpen Your Math

A short Grade 5 refresher for New York students before you practice

Place Value and Rounding

- In 348,726, the digit 8 is in the thousands place, so its value is 8,000.
- Expanded form: $348{,}726 = 300{,}000 + 40{,}000 + 8{,}000 + 700 + 20 + 6$
- To round to a place value, look at the digit to the right of that place.
- Example: 62,849 rounded to the nearest thousand is 63,000.

Order of Operations

Use this order:

1. parentheses
2. multiplication and division from left to right
3. addition and subtraction from left to right

$$18-2\times(3+4) = 18-2\times7 = 18-14 = 4$$

A New York Word Problem

Niagara Falls drops about 167 ft. A platform descends 92 ft, then 58 ft. How much further to the river?

Show your work clearly. Estimate first if it helps. Check labels and units before circling a final answer.

Helpful reminder: line up place values when adding or subtracting large numbers and decimals. Straight columns make checking much easier.

Fractions and Decimals

Fraction Facts

- numerator = how many equal parts you have
- denominator = how many equal parts make one whole
- equivalent fractions name the same amount

$$\frac{2}{3} = \frac{4}{6} = \frac{8}{12}$$

Add and Subtract Fractions

When denominators match, work with the numerators.

$$\frac{5}{8} + \frac{2}{8} = \frac{7}{8}$$

$$\frac{9}{10} - \frac{4}{10} = \frac{5}{10} = \frac{1}{2}$$

Multiply a Fraction by a Whole Number

$$4 \times \frac{3}{5} = \frac{12}{5} = 2\frac{2}{5}$$

This is repeated addition:

$$\frac{3}{5} + \frac{3}{5} + \frac{3}{5} + \frac{3}{5}$$

Decimal Place Value

In 3.472, the 3 is in the ones place, the 4 is in the tenths, the 7 is in the hundredths, and the 2 is in the thousandths.

$$0.5 = \frac{1}{2} \qquad 0.25 = \frac{1}{4} \qquad 0.6 = \frac{3}{5}$$

Compare carefully: with like denominators, compare numerators. With decimals, compare the whole-number part first, then tenths, then hundredths, then thousandths.

Measurement and Geometry

Perimeter, Area, and Volume

Perimeter is the distance around a figure.

$$P = 2l + 2w$$

Area measures the space inside a rectangle.

$$A = l \times w$$

Volume measures the space inside a rectangular prism.

$$V = l \times w \times h$$

If $l = 10$, $w = 3$, and $h = 4$, then $P = 26$ units, $A = 30$ square units, $V = 120$ cubic units.

Angles and Lines

- right angle = exactly 90°
- acute angle = less than 90°
- obtuse angle = more than 90° and less than 180°
- parallel lines never meet
- perpendicular lines meet at a right angle

A point on the coordinate plane is written as (x, y). For example, $(2, 5)$ means 2 across and 5 up.

Units matter: length uses units like inches or centimeters, area uses square units, and volume uses cubic units.

Data and Problem Solving

Tables and Graphs

- read the title and labels first
- check the scale before comparing values
- line plots often show fractions
- tables can reveal patterns and rules

Numerical Patterns

Look for what changes each time.

3, 7, 11, 15

This pattern adds 4 each step.

4, 8, 16, 32

This pattern multiplies by 2 each step.

A Strong Plan for Word Problems

1. Read the problem twice.
2. Decide what you need to find.
3. Choose the operation, model, table, or pattern that fits best.
4. Solve step by step.
5. Check with an estimate or with the opposite operation when possible.

Final reminder for New York mathematicians: a quick review is not a race. It is a reset that helps you walk into the test ready to think clearly.

New York Grade 5 Math Standards Reference

This rewritten guide presents the Grade 5 mathematics expectations for New York, aligned to New York Next Generation Mathematics Learning Standards. The official standard code stays on the left; the explanation on the right restates the same expectation in new, classroom-friendly language.

5.G | Geometry

Students connect geometry with location by sorting plane figures according to their attributes and using coordinate grids to represent points.

5.G.1	This standard asks students to use a pair of perpendicular number lines, called axes, to define a coordinate system, with the intersection of the lines (the origin) arranged to coincide with the 0 on each line and a given point in the plane located by using a coordinate pair of numbers, called its coordinates. Understand that the first number indicates how far to travel from the origin in the direction of one axis, and the second number indicates how far to travel in the direction of the second axis, with the convention that the names of the two axes and the coordinates correspond.
5.G.2	The learning target is for students to represent real world and mathematical problems by graphing points in the first quadrant of the coordinate grid, and interpret coordinate values of points in the context of the situation.
5.G.3	Students explain that when a property belongs to a larger shape category, every more specific subcategory also has that property.
5.G.4	Students arrange plane figures in a hierarchy, showing how broader shape groups contain more specific groups.

5.MD | Measurement and Data

Students change units within a measurement system, make sense of data displays, and build an understanding of volume.

5.MD.1	The learning target is for students to convert among different-sized standard measurement units within a given measurement system when the conversion factor is given. Use these conversions in solving multi-part, real world problems.
5.MD.2	Students demonstrate understanding as they make a line plot to display a set of data of measurements in fractions of a unit (1/2, 1/4, 1/8). Use operations on fractions for this grade to solve problems involving information presented in line plots.

5.MD.3 Students see volume as a measurable feature of solid figures and explain how cubic units are used to measure it.

5.MD.4 This standard asks students to measure volumes by counting unit cubes, using cubic cm, cubic in., cubic ft., and improvised units.

5.MD.5 The learning target is for students to relate volume to the operations of multiplication and addition and solve real world and mathematical problems involving volume.

5.MD.3a Students demonstrate understanding as they recognize that a cube with side length 1 unit, called a "unit cube," is said to have "one cubic unit" of volume, and can be used to measure volume.

5.MD.3b Students should be able to recognize that a solid figure which can be packed without gaps or overlaps usingnunit cubes is said to have a volume ofncubic units.

5.MD.5a This standard asks students to find the volume of a right rectangular prism with whole-number side lengths by packing it with unit cubes, and show that the volume is the same as would be found by multiplying the edge lengths, equivalently by multiplying the height by the area of the base.

5.MD.5b The learning target is for students to apply the formulas$V=l\times w\times h$and$V=B\times h$for rectangular prisms to find volumes of right rectangular prisms with whole-number edge lengths in the context of solving real world and mathematical problems.

5.MD.5c Students demonstrate understanding as they recognize volume as additive. Find volumes of solid figures composed of two non-overlapping right rectangular prisms by adding the volumes of the non-overlapping parts, applying this technique to solve real world problems.

5.NBT | Number and Operations in Base Ten

Students use base-ten structure to reason about large whole numbers and decimals, then apply that reasoning while calculating.

5.NBT.1 This standard asks students to recognize that in a multi-digit number, a digit in one place represents 10 times as much as it represents in the place to its right and 1/10 of what it represents in the place to its left.

5.NBT.2 The learning target is for students to use whole-number exponents to denote powers of 10. Explain patterns in the number of zeros of the product when multiplying a number by powers of 10, and explain patterns in the placement of the decimal point when a decimal is multiplied or divided by a power of 10.

5.NBT.3 Students work with decimals through the thousandths place by reading values, writing them in different forms, and comparing their sizes.

5.NBT.4 Students round decimal numbers to a named place by using the value of nearby digits and the size of the number.

5.NBT.5 This standard asks students to fluently multiply whole numbers with several digits using a standard calculation algorithm.

5.NBT.6 Students divide whole numbers with dividends up to four digits and two-digit divisors, using place value, operation properties, and multiplication-division relationships; they justify their work with equations, arrays, or area models.

5.NBT.7 Students demonstrate understanding as they using concrete models or drawings and strategies based on place value, operation properties, and/or the relationship between operations: add and subtract decimals to hundredths; multiply and divide decimals to hundredths. Relate the strategy to a written method and explain the reasoning used.

5.NBT.3a Students should be able to read and write decimals to thousandths using base-ten numerals, number names, and expanded form.

5.NBT.3b This standard asks students to compare two decimals to thousandths based on meanings of the digits in each place, using $>$, $=$, and $<$ symbols to record the results of comparisons.

5.NF | Number and Operations—Fractions

This section focuses on number and Operations—Fractions.

5.NF.1 Students add and subtract fractions, including mixed numbers, by creating equivalent fractions with common denominators before combining or comparing the amounts.

5.NF.2 Students should be able to solve word problems involving addition and subtraction of fractions referring to the same whole, including cases of unlike denominators. Use friendly benchmark fractions and number sense of fractions to estimate mentally and assess the reasonableness of answers.

5.NF.3 This standard asks students to interpret a fraction as division of the numerator by the denominator (a/b=a÷b). Solve word problems involving division of whole numbers leading to answers in the form of fractions or mixed numbers.

5.NF.4 Students extend multiplication ideas so they can multiply fractions by whole numbers and multiply fractions by fractions.

5.NF.5 Students demonstrate understanding as they interpret multiplication as scaling (resizing).

5.NF.6 Students should be able to solve real world problems involving multiplication of fractions and mixed numbers.

5.NF.7 Students extend division ideas to situations involving unit fractions divided by whole numbers and whole numbers divided by unit fractions.

5.NF.4a The learning target is for students to interpret the product (a/b) ×qasaparts of a partition ofqintobequal parts; equivalently, as the result of a sequence of operationsa×q÷b.

5.NF.4b Students demonstrate understanding as they find the area of a rectangle with fractional side lengths by tiling it with rectangles of the appropriate unit fraction side lengths, and show that the area is the same as would be found by multiplying the side lengths. Multiply fractional side lengths to find areas of rectangles, and represent fraction products as rectangular areas.

5.NF.5a Students should be able to compare the size of a product to the size of one factor on the basis of the size of the other factor, without performing the indicated multiplication.

5.NF.5b This standard asks students to explain why multiplying a given number by a fraction greater than 1 results in a product greater than the given number (recognizing multiplication by whole numbers greater than 1 as a familiar case). Explain why multiplying a given number by a fraction less than 1 results in a product smaller than the given number. Relate the principle of fraction equivalencea/b= (n×a)/(n×b) to the effect of multiplyinga/bby 1.

5.NF.7a The learning target is for students to interpret division of a unit fraction by a non-zero whole number, and compute such quotients.

5.NF.7b Students demonstrate understanding as they interpret division of a whole number by a unit fraction, and compute such quotients.

5.NF.7c Students should be able to solve real-life problems involving division of unit fractions by non-zero whole numbers and division of whole numbers by unit fractions.

5.OA | Operations and Algebraic Thinking

Students use numbers, symbols, and rules to describe calculations, explain expressions, and investigate patterns between related quantities.

5.OA.1 The learning target is for students to apply the order of operations to evaluate numerical expressions.

5.OA.2 Students write numerical expressions to show calculations and explain what those expressions mean without needing to compute the final value.

5.OA.3 Students build two number patterns from given rules, compare matching terms, create coordinate pairs, and plot those pairs on a coordinate grid.

Table of Contents

Grade 5 Math

Grade 5 Mathematics

Questions: 40 **Duration:** No time limit

Calculator Policy: Calculators are not allowed

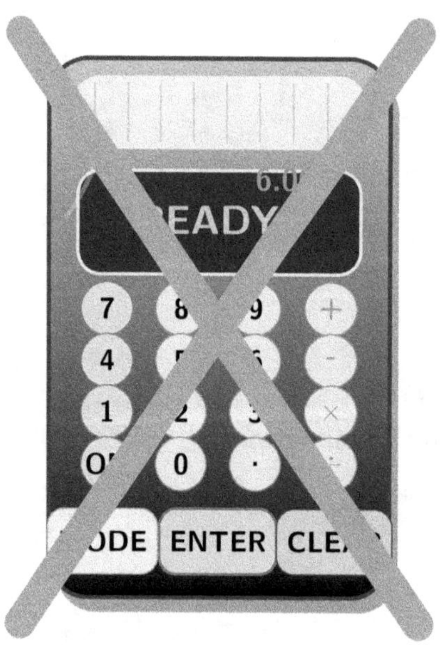

Grade 5 Mathematics Reference Materials

PERIMETER AND AREA

Perimeter of Rectangle	$P = 2l + 2w$ or $P = 2(l + w)$
Area of Rectangle	$A = l \times w$
Area of Triangle	$A = \frac{1}{2} \times b \times h$
Volume of Rectangular Prism	$V = l \times w \times h$

LENGTH

Customary	Metric
1 foot (ft) = 12 inches (in.)	1 meter (m) = 100 centimeters (cm)
1 yard (yd) = 3 feet (ft)	1 centimeter (cm) = 10 millimeters (mm)
1 yard (yd) = 36 inches (in.)	1 kilometer (km) = 1,000 meters (m)

CAPACITY

Customary	Metric
1 cup (c) = 8 fluid ounces (fl oz)	1 liter (L) = 1,000 milliliters (mL)
1 pint (pt) = 2 cups (c)	
1 quart (qt) = 2 pints (pt)	
1 gallon (gal) = 4 quarts (qt)	

WEIGHT AND MASS

Customary	Metric
1 pound (lb) = 16 ounces (oz)	1 kilogram (kg) = 1,000 grams (g)
	1 gram (g) = 1,000 milligrams (mg)

TIME

1 minute (min) = 60 seconds (sec)	1 week = 7 days
1 hour (hr) = 60 minutes (min)	1 year = 12 months
1 day = 24 hours (hr)	1 year = 52 weeks

1) A trail is divided into $\frac{1}{3}$-mile segments. How many segments are in 3 miles?

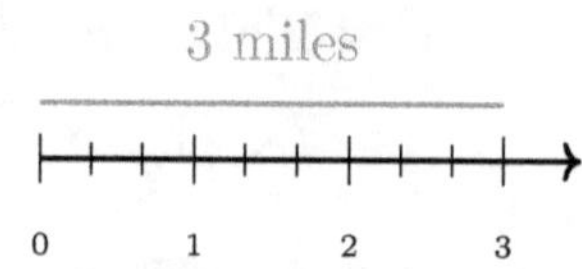

Each mile is split into thirds.

☐ A. 3
☐ B. 6
☐ C. 9
☐ D. 12

2) Which expression represents a number with the digit 5 in the ten-thousands place?

☐ A. 5×10^3
☐ B. 5×10^1
☐ C. 5×10^2
☐ D. 5×10^4

3) Three identical rectangular prisms each have dimensions 4 in $\times$ 5 in $\times$ 3 in. What is the total volume of all three?

☐ A. 180 in^3
☐ B. 240 in^3
☐ C. 300 in^3
☐ D. 360 in^3

4) One sixth of a chocolate bar is split among 5 friends. Which division equation finds each share?

☐ A. $5 \div \frac{1}{6} = n$
☐ B. $\frac{1}{6} \times 5 = n$
☐ C. $\frac{1}{6} \div 5 = n$
☐ D. $5 + \frac{1}{6} = n$

5) The line plot shows the heights (in half-inches) of plant seedlings in a garden:

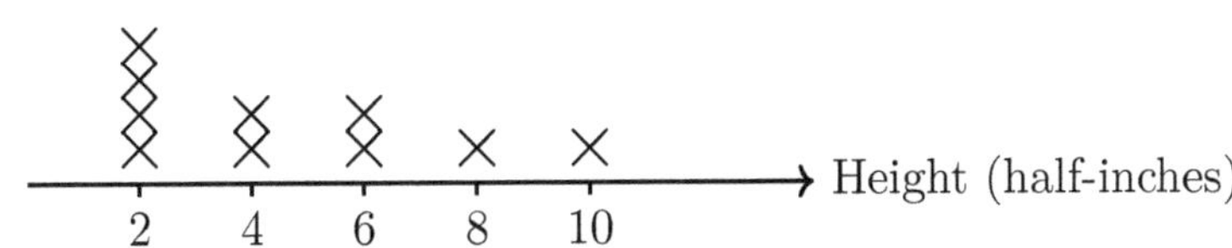

What is the total height of all seedlings in inches?

☐ A. 21 inches
☐ B. 22 inches
☐ C. 23 inches
☐ D. 24 inches

6) A strip shows one eighth split into 3 equal parts. Which equation matches the model?

☐ A. $3 \div \frac{1}{8} = ?$
☐ B. $\frac{1}{8} \times 3 = ?$
☐ C. $\frac{1}{8} \div 3 = ?$
☐ D. $3 + \frac{1}{8} = ?$

7) Tailor has two cloth pieces: $3\frac{2}{5}$ yd and $2\frac{3}{5}$ yd. Total?

☐ A. 5 yd
☐ B. 6 yd
☐ C. $6\frac{1}{5}$ yd
☐ D. $6\frac{3}{5}$ yd

8) Find: $0.4 \div 10$.

Record your answer in the space provided.

9) Two rectangular prisms have the same base dimensions of 3 in. × 4 in. Prism A is 5 inches tall, and Prism B is 3 inches tall. What is the difference in their volumes?

Prism A	Prism B
$3 \times 4 \times 5$ in.	$3 \times 4 \times 3$ in.

☐ A. 12 cubic in.
☐ B. 60 cubic in.
☐ C. 36 cubic in.
☐ D. 24 cubic in.

10) A student needs to compare $\frac{7}{10}$ and $\frac{4}{9}$. She first lists multiples of 10 and 9 to find the LCD. What is the least common denominator?

Multiples

Multiples of 10: 10, 20, 30, 40, 50, 60, 70, 80, 90

Multiples of 9: 9, 18, 27, 36, 45, 54, 63, 72, 81, 90

First common:

☐ A. 19
☐ B. 45
☐ C. 90
☐ D. 180

11) A classroom cubby has volume 128 cubic inches. Its base is 8 inches by 4 inches. What is its height?

☐ A. 3 inches
☐ B. 4 inches
☐ C. 5 inches
☐ D. 32 inches

12) Pattern A: $0, 3, 6, 9, \ldots$. Pattern B: $0, 9, 18, 27, \ldots$. For the nonzero terms, each B value is how many times the matching A value?

Record your answer in the space provided.

13) The fraction bar shows $\frac{1}{6}$ of a meter. This length is shared equally among 2 people. How much does each person get?

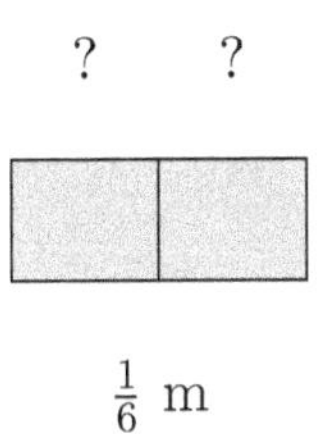

☐ A. $\frac{1}{3}$ m
☐ B. $\frac{1}{12}$ m
☐ C. $\frac{1}{6}$ m
☐ D. $\frac{1}{4}$ m

14) Without calculating, compare $12 \times \frac{5}{3}$ to 12. Which is true?

☐ A. $12 \times \frac{5}{3} < 12$
☐ B. $12 \times \frac{5}{3} = 12$
☐ C. $12 \times \frac{5}{3} > 12$
☐ D. Cannot be compared

15)

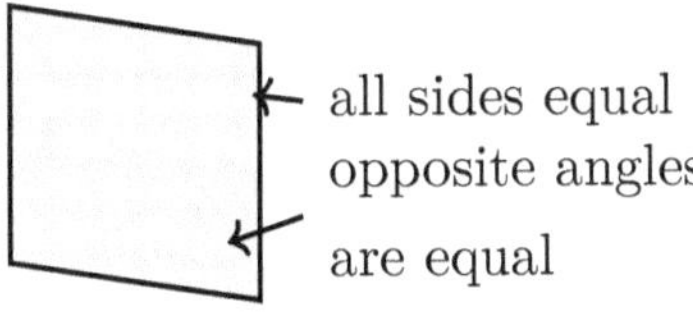

What is the BEST name for this figure?

☐ A. Parallelogram
☐ B. Rhombus
☐ C. Rectangle
☐ D. Trapezoid

16) On this coordinate plane, which point is located at $(9, 1)$?

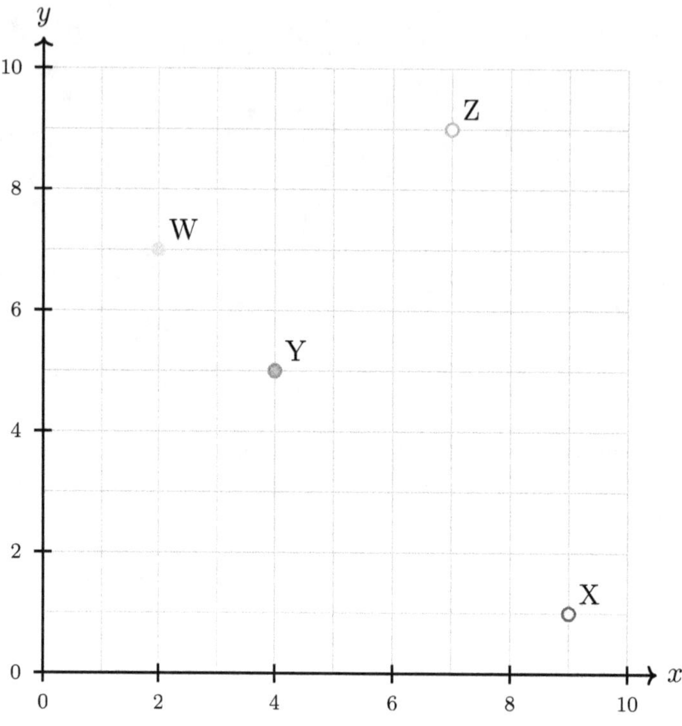

☐ A. Point W
☐ B. Point X
☐ C. Point Y
☐ D. Point Z

17) Which fraction is equivalent to $\frac{3}{5}$?

☐ A. $\frac{5}{3}$
☐ B. $\frac{3}{15}$
☐ C. $\frac{4}{5}$
☐ D. $\frac{6}{10}$

18) Which numbers round to 3.2 when rounded to the nearest tenth? *Select all that apply.*

☐ A. 3.17
☐ B. 3.24
☐ C. 3.25
☐ D. 3.09

19) Which two prisms have the same volume?

Prism	Length	Width	Height
P	5	4	6
Q	10	3	5
R	8	6	2
S	4	4	6

☐ A. P and Q
☐ B. Q and R
☐ C. R and S
☐ D. P and S

20) A piece of ribbon is $\frac{5}{6}$ yard long. Mia cuts off $\frac{3}{8}$ yard. How much ribbon is left?

☐ A. $\frac{1}{24}$ yard
☐ B. $\frac{5}{24}$ yard
☐ C. $\frac{11}{24}$ yard
☐ D. $\frac{7}{12}$ yard

21) Rosa uses two number patterns to create ordered pairs. Pattern 1 uses 5, 10, 15, 20. Pattern 2 uses 2, 4, 6, 8. What ordered pair is first?

☐ A. (2, 5)
☐ B. (10, 4)
☐ C. (20, 8)
☐ D. (5, 2)

22) To get a product that ends in exactly 2 zeros, which number must go in the blank?

$$\_\_\_ \times 200 = \text{product ending in exactly 2 zeros}$$

☐ A. 15
☐ B. 50
☐ C. 5,000
☐ D. 3

23) What is 5.6×1.5?

☐ A. 8.1
☐ B. 8.3
☐ C. 8.4
☐ D. 9.1

24) Which is the best estimate for $823 \div 41$?

☐ A. 20
☐ B. 15
☐ C. 25
☐ D. 30

25) Which statement about triangles is true?

☐ A. An equilateral triangle has three equal sides.
☐ B. A scalene triangle has two equal sides.
☐ C. Every right triangle has three equal sides.
☐ D. Every triangle has a right angle.

26) A solid is built with 5 equal layers. Each layer has 12 unit cubes. What is the total volume?

Record your answer in the space provided.

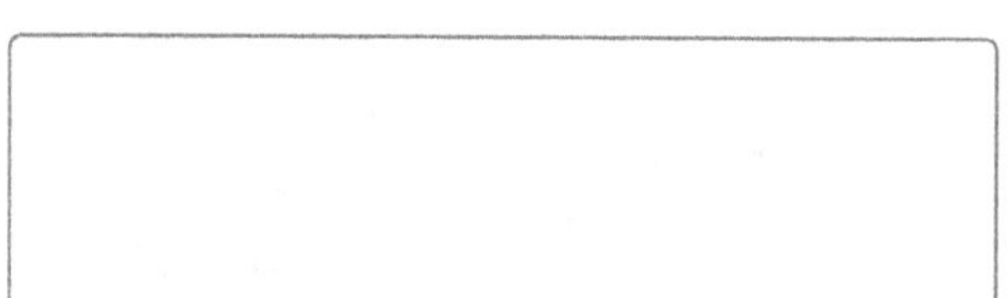

27) How many ounces are in 4 pounds?

4 lb ⟶ ? ounces

(1 lb = 16 oz)

☐ A. 16 ounces
☐ B. 32 ounces
☐ C. 48 ounces
☐ D. 64 ounces

28) Find: 250×10^2.

Record your answer in the space provided.

29) The line plot shows bean plant growth (in centimeters) for 11 students' projects:

Bean Plant Heights

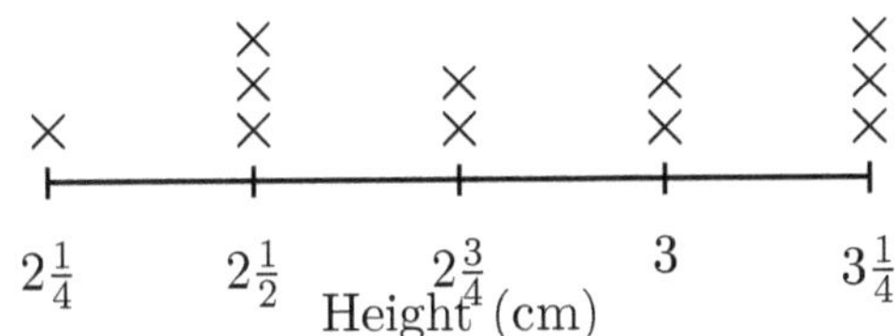

Which height is the least common?

☐ A. $2\frac{1}{4}$ cm

☐ B. $2\frac{1}{2}$ cm

☐ C. $2\frac{3}{4}$ cm

☐ D. 3 cm

30) On a graph, two stores are plotted at $(7,5)$ and $(2,5)$. How many blocks east or west apart are the stores?

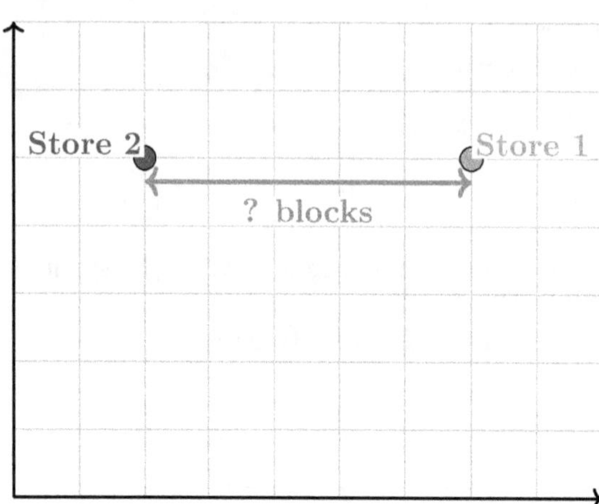

☐ A. 3 blocks
☐ B. 4 blocks
☐ C. 5 blocks
☐ D. 7 blocks

31) A drink recipe makes 8 servings and requires 2 cups 4 fluid ounces of juice. To make 2 servings, how much juice is needed?
Use: 1 cup = 8 fluid ounces

☐ A. 12 fluid ounces
☐ B. 7 fluid ounces
☐ C. 10 fluid ounces
☐ D. 5 fluid ounces

32)

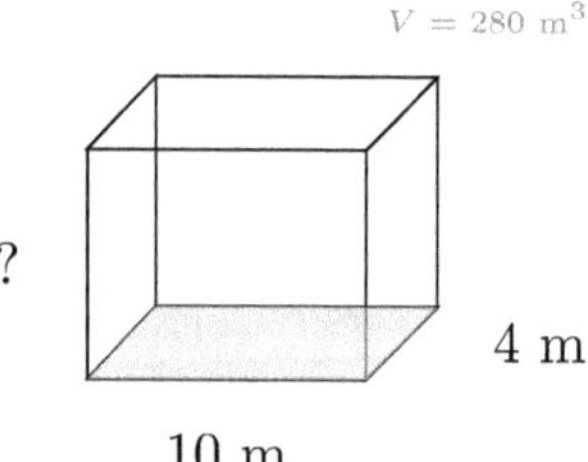

Find the missing dimension (height).

☐ A. 7 m
☐ B. 266 m
☐ C. 294 m
☐ D. 70 m

33) Expanded form using multiplication by powers of 10: $2 \times 1 + 3 \times \frac{1}{10} + 7 \times \frac{1}{100}$ equals which decimal?

☐ A. 2.37
☐ B. 2.73
☐ C. 237
☐ D. 0.237

34) Which number is least: 0.6, 0.55, or 0.605?

Record your answer in the space provided.

35) Evaluate: $72 \div 8 + 3 \times 3 - 5$

☐ A. 12
☐ B. 13
☐ C. 14
☐ D. 16

36) A water tank holds 50 liters. A leak drains $\frac{3}{10}$ of the water. How many liters are drained?

☐ A. 5 liters
☐ B. 10 liters
☐ C. 35 liters
☐ D. 15 liters

37) A science lab measures a sample with a mass of 15.375 grams. What is the digit in the hundredths place?

☐ A. 1
☐ B. 3
☐ C. 7
☐ D. 5

38) A composite solid is made from two non-overlapping prisms. One prism measures 8 cm by 3 cm by 4 cm, and the other measures 5 cm by 3 cm by 4 cm. Which expression finds the total volume?

☐ A. $8+3+4+5+3+4$
☐ B. $(8\times 5)+(3\times 4)$
☐ C. $8\times 5\times 4$
☐ D. $(8\times 3\times 4)+(5\times 3\times 4)$

39) What is 0.36×10 as a decimal?

☐ A. 0.36
☐ B. 36
☐ C. 0.036
☐ D. 3.6

40) Where should parentheses be placed to make the expression equal 20?

$$6+4\times 2$$

☐ A. $(6+4)\times 2$
☐ B. $6+(4\times 2)$
☐ C. $6\times(4+2)$
☐ D. $(6\times 4)+2$

End of Practice Test

Take a short breath, then check your work with care. Good corrections can teach almost as much as the test itself.

What-If Wizard! ✓

You finished a full test. That takes focus and stamina.
"What if?" is a magic phrase in math.

What If? Unlocks the Answer ★

Lucas loved asking "what if?" "What if I tried a smaller number first? What if I drew this differently? What if I worked backwards?"

Each "what if?" was a small experiment. Most failed, but each one taught him something. Eventually, one worked.

On 5th grade tests, when you're stuck, run a quick "what if" experiment. A wrong attempt teaches you what's right.

Math Mindset Tip: **Stuck? Try a what-if. Even a wrong attempt narrows the path.**

Every "what if?" is a step toward the answer.
— Math Mindset

Lucas's Amazing Journey ★

Lucas wasn't afraid to be wrong. He knew that being wrong on a tiny experiment was much cheaper than being wrong on the real problem.
Imagine you're stuck on a fraction problem. "What if I used $\frac{1}{2}$ instead of the actual fraction?" If you can solve the simpler one, the path is clearer.
Try Lucas's habit: when stuck, swap in friendlier numbers, solve the smaller version, and then return to the original.

Lucas's Secret: **Test your idea on a smaller problem first.**

Try this on your next practice test. Small, smart habits become big score boosters.

★ Ask "what if?" Then test it. ★

Brave guesses (with checking) lead to right answers.

Grade 5 Mathematics

Questions: 40 **Duration:** No time limit

Calculator Policy: Calculators are not allowed

Grade 5 Mathematics Reference Materials

PERIMETER AND AREA

Perimeter of Rectangle	$P = 2l + 2w$ or $P = 2(l + w)$
Area of Rectangle	$A = l \times w$
Area of Triangle	$A = \frac{1}{2} \times b \times h$
Volume of Rectangular Prism	$V = l \times w \times h$

LENGTH

Customary	**Metric**
1 foot (ft) = 12 inches (in.)	1 meter (m) = 100 centimeters (cm)
1 yard (yd) = 3 feet (ft)	1 centimeter (cm) = 10 millimeters (mm)
1 yard (yd) = 36 inches (in.)	1 kilometer (km) = 1,000 meters (m)

CAPACITY

Customary	**Metric**
1 cup (c) = 8 fluid ounces (fl oz)	1 liter (L) = 1,000 milliliters (mL)
1 pint (pt) = 2 cups (c)	
1 quart (qt) = 2 pints (pt)	
1 gallon (gal) = 4 quarts (qt)	

WEIGHT AND MASS

Customary	**Metric**
1 pound (lb) = 16 ounces (oz)	1 kilogram (kg) = 1,000 grams (g)
	1 gram (g) = 1,000 milligrams (mg)

TIME

1 minute (min) = 60 seconds (sec)	1 week = 7 days
1 hour (hr) = 60 minutes (min)	1 year = 12 months
1 day = 24 hours (hr)	1 year = 52 weeks

1) A restaurant receives 936 napkins delivered in packs of 13. How many full packs?

☐ A. 70
☐ B. 72
☐ C. 74
☐ D. 76

2) Add: $\frac{2}{7} + \frac{3}{4}$

☐ A. $\frac{5}{11}$
☐ B. $\frac{29}{28}$
☐ C. $\frac{5}{28}$
☐ D. $\frac{8}{28}$

3) A gift box is a rectangular prism with volume 240 cm^3. The base measures 8 cm by 6 cm. What is the height?

☐ A. 5 cm
☐ B. 4 cm
☐ C. 3 cm
☐ D. 6 cm

4) Pattern: $10, 20, 40, 80, \ldots$ Which rule describes it?

☐ A. Add 10 each time
☐ B. Add previous two terms
☐ C. Multiply by 3
☐ D. Multiply by 2 each time

5) Which pair of expressions have the same value?

☐ A. 3,000 ÷ 10 and 300 ÷ 10
☐ B. 2,100 ÷ 100 and 210 ÷ 10
☐ C. 5,600 ÷ 1,000 and 56 ÷ 100
☐ D. 1,500 ÷ 100 and 1,500 ÷ 1,000

6) A strip of paper is 12 inches long. Another strip is $2\frac{1}{2}$ times as long. How long is the longer strip?

☐ A. 42 inches
☐ B. 36 inches
☐ C. 24 inches
☐ D. 30 inches

7) During a class field trip, 28 students and 4 adults travel by bus. The bus has 40 seats. How many empty seats are there?

☐ A. 12 seats
☐ B. 6 seats
☐ C. 10 seats
☐ D. 8 seats

8) Pattern R: 10, 20, 30, 40. Pattern S: 2, 4, 6, 8. Use the matched values to express R in terms of S.

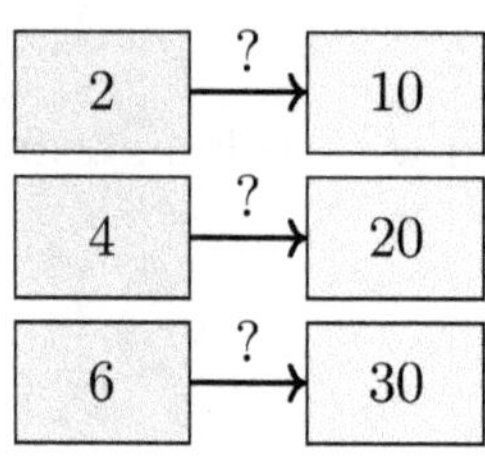

☐ A. R is 5 times S
☐ B. R is 8 more than S
☐ C. R is 3 times S, then 4 more
☐ D. R is twice S, then 6 more

9) What is 214×2?

☐ A. 418
☐ B. 428
☐ C. 438
☐ D. 448

10) Three points lie on the same horizontal grid line, 5 units above the x-axis. What can be true about their first coordinates?

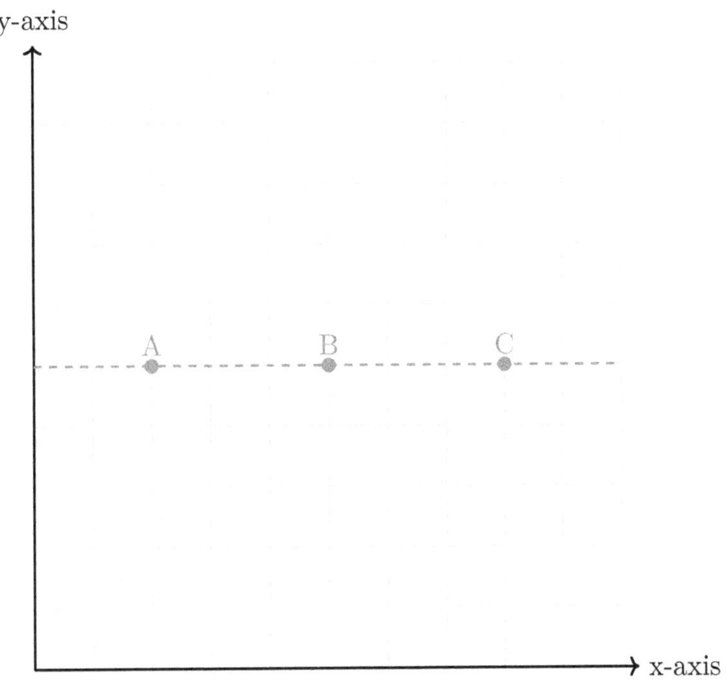

☐ A. They are all the same
☐ B. They must be 0
☐ C. They must be 5
☐ D. They can be different

11) Compare the two expressions without evaluating: $7 \times 25 + 7 \times 5$ and $7 \times (25 + 5)$.

☐ A. First is larger
☐ B. Second is larger
☐ C. Equal
☐ D. Cannot tell

12) A distance is 15 kilometers. If 1 km = 10^3 meters, how many meters?

☐ A. 150 meters
☐ B. 1500 meters
☐ C. 15000 meters
☐ D. 150000 meters

13) A sandwich shop earned \$189.00 from turkey sandwiches and \$206.50 from ham sandwiches in one day. What was the total revenue?

Record your answer in the space provided.

14) Compare without calculating: $(55 + 17)$ and $(55 + 17) \div 2$.

- ☐ A. The first is twice the second
- ☐ B. The first is half the second
- ☐ C. The first is the same
- ☐ D. The first is 2 less

15) A child is 1.35 meters tall. How many centimeters is that?

- ☐ A. 13.5 cm
- ☐ B. 135 cm
- ☐ C. 1,350 cm
- ☐ D. 13,500 cm

16) One tenth of a poster is shared equally by 2 students. Which division equation finds each share?

- ☐ A. $\frac{1}{10} \div 2 = n$
- ☐ B. $2 \div \frac{1}{10} = n$
- ☐ C. $\frac{1}{10} \times 2 = n$
- ☐ D. $2 + \frac{1}{10} = n$

17) Find: $\frac{5}{6} \times \frac{3}{10}$.

Record your answer in the space provided.

18) $720 \div 100 =?$

☐ A. 0.72
☐ B. 7.2
☐ C. 72
☐ D. 720

19) Find: $\frac{4}{5} \times 15$.

Record your answer in the space provided.

20) A small closet has dimensions 3 feet by 2 feet by 8 feet. A larger closet has dimensions 4 feet by 3 feet by 8 feet. What is the difference in volume between them?

Small closet	Larger closet
$3 \times 2 \times 8$ ft	$4 \times 3 \times 8$ ft

☐ A. 8 cubic feet
☐ B. 12 cubic feet
☐ C. 48 cubic feet
☐ D. 96 cubic feet

21) Maya walked $\frac{3}{4}$ mile and then $\frac{1}{2}$ mile. Which statements are true? *Select all that apply.*

☐ A. Total distance is $1\frac{1}{4}$ miles.
☐ B. She walked more than 1 mile in total.
☐ C. Total distance is $\frac{3}{8}$ mile.
☐ D. She walked less than $\frac{3}{4}$ mile in total.

22) 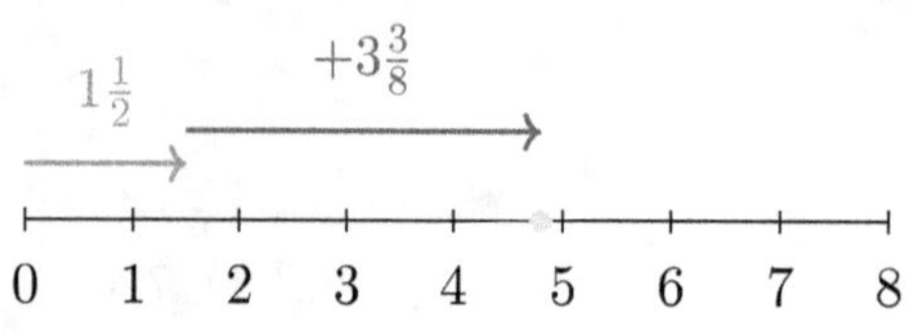

Number line: $1\frac{1}{2} + 3\frac{3}{8} = ?$

☐ A. $4\frac{7}{8}$
☐ B. $4\frac{3}{4}$
☐ C. 5
☐ D. $5\frac{1}{8}$

23) What is the least common multiple of 4 and 6?

☐ A. 10
☐ B. 4
☐ C. 24
☐ D. 12

24) Estimate: $\frac{11}{12} - \frac{2}{7}$.

☐ A. Close to 0
☐ B. Close to $\frac{1}{2}$
☐ C. Close to 1
☐ D. Close to $\frac{3}{2}$

25) A shipping crate measures 10 centimeters long, 3 centimeters wide, and 4 centimeters tall. What is its volume?

☐ A. 120 cubic centimeters
☐ B. 30 cubic centimeters
☐ C. 40 cubic centimeters
☐ D. 12 cubic centimeters

26) Which polygon has 8 sides and 8 vertices?

☐ A. Pentagon
☐ B. Hexagon
☐ C. Octagon
☐ D. Nonagon

27) Three identical, non-overlapping prisms are stacked to form a larger rectangular solid. Each prism is 3 cm × 4 cm × 2 cm, and all three prisms are included. What is the total volume?

3 identical prisms stacked
each 3 cm × 4 cm × 2 cm

☐ A. 48 cm^3

☐ B. 72 cm^3

☐ C. 96 cm^3

☐ D. 120 cm^3

28) A paint can is $\frac{5}{8}$ full. You use $\frac{2}{5}$ of the paint in the can. What fraction of a full can did you use?

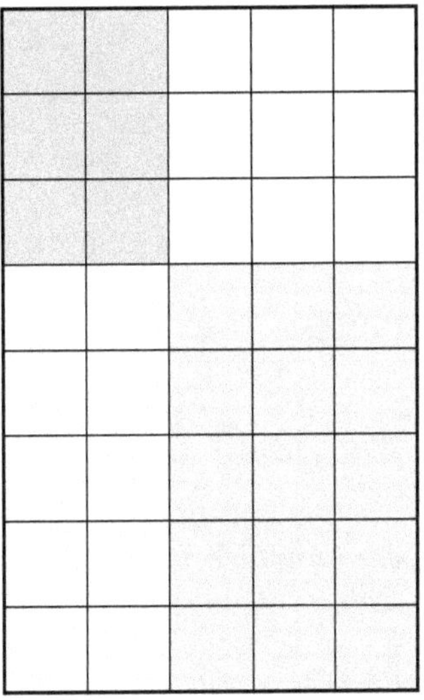

☐ A. $\frac{3}{13}$

☐ B. $\frac{1}{5}$

☐ C. $\frac{2}{5}$

☐ D. $\frac{10}{40}$ or $\frac{1}{4}$

29) Order these four decimals from least to greatest:

6.02, 6.18, 6.5, 6.35

☐ A. 6.02, 6.18, 6.35, 6.5

☐ B. 6.02, 6.35, 6.18, 6.5

☐ C. 6.5, 6.35, 6.18, 6.02

☐ D. 6.18, 6.02, 6.35, 6.5

30) A tank holds 9.5 gallons. After draining 4.07 gallons, how much remains?

- ☐ A. 5.53 gal
- ☐ B. 4.98 gal
- ☐ C. 5.33 gal
- ☐ D. 5.43 gal

31) A science experiment measures 7.635 grams. Round to nearest hundredth.

- ☐ A. 7.6 g
- ☐ B. 7.63 g
- ☐ C. 7.64 g
- ☐ D. 7.7 g

32) A board is $\frac{5}{6}$ m long. Three identical boards are joined end to end. What is the total length?

Record your answer in the space provided.

33) A baker has 5 pounds of flour. Each loaf needs $\frac{1}{4}$ pound. How many loaves can be made?

Record your answer in the space provided.

34) A school divided 52.3 kg of flour equally among 10 classrooms. How much flour did each classroom get?

- ☐ A. 523 kg
- ☐ B. 5.23 kg
- ☐ C. 0.523 kg
- ☐ D. 52.3 kg

35) The line plot shows ounces of juice in different bottles:

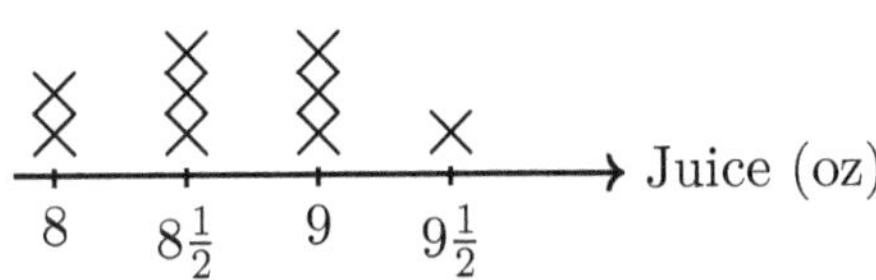

How many ounces of juice are in all the bottles?

☐ A. 78 oz
☐ B. 76 oz
☐ C. 80 oz
☐ D. 84 oz

36) What is 78×100?

☐ A. 780
☐ B. 708
☐ C. 78,000
☐ D. 7,800

37) What are the dimensions of a rectangular prism that contains exactly 36 unit cubes?

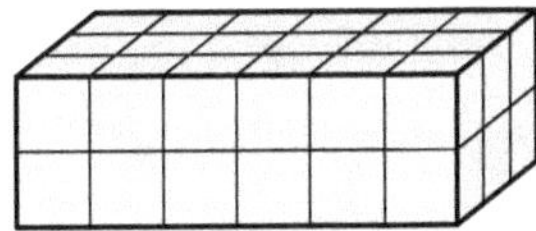

☐ A. $2 \times 2 \times 8$
☐ B. $2 \times 3 \times 6$
☐ C. $3 \times 4 \times 2$
☐ D. $3 \times 3 \times 5$

38) Which pair of expressions has the same value?

☐ A. $3 \times (4 + 5)$ and $3 \times 4 + 5$
☐ B. $2 \times (10 - 3)$ and $2 \times 10 - 3$
☐ C. $4 \times (6 + 2)$ and $4 \times 6 + 4 \times 2$
☐ D. $5 + (3 \times 7)$ and $(5 + 3) \times 7$

39) Which student made an error subtracting $5\frac{1}{4} - 2\frac{3}{4}$?

Student	Work	Answer
A	Borrow 1: $4\frac{5}{4} - 2\frac{3}{4}$	$2\frac{2}{4} = 2\frac{1}{2}$
B	Subtract whole parts and fraction parts separately	$3\frac{2}{4}$
C	Convert: $\frac{21}{4} - \frac{11}{4}$	$\frac{10}{4} = 2\frac{1}{2}$
D	Count up from $2\frac{3}{4}$ to $5\frac{1}{4}$	$2\frac{1}{2}$

☐ A. Student A
☐ B. Student B
☐ C. Student C
☐ D. Student D

40) The output is 4 more than the input. What is the 5th ordered pair if the inputs start at 1?

☐ A. $(4, 8)$
☐ B. $(5, 9)$
☐ C. $(6, 10)$
☐ D. $(5, 1)$

End of Practice Test

Take a short breath, then check your work with care. Good corrections can teach almost as much as the test itself.

Precision Champion!

You finished a full test. That takes focus and stamina.

Almost-right is still wrong. Train your eyes to see exactly.

Precision Beats Almost-Right

Mei loved math, but she sometimes lost points for tiny mistakes: a missing zero, a wrong decimal, a flipped negative.

She started a new habit: "finger-trace" the numbers she copied. With one finger on the page and her eyes following, she copied every digit exactly. The careless mistakes vanished.

On 5th grade tests, exact copying is a superpower. Numbers in the question must match numbers in your work. One small change, one wrong answer.

Math Mindset Tip: **Copy numbers carefully. Touch them with your eyes (or a fingertip).**

Precision turns hard work into the right answer.

— Math Mindset

Mei's Amazing Journey ★

Mei's secret wasn't speed. It was care. After she copied a number from the question to her work, she paused and read it back to make sure it matched.
Imagine a problem with 1,204. If you write 1,240 instead, every step after that is wrong—even when the math is perfect.
Try Mei's check on the next test. Two seconds of care can save four big points.

Mei's Secret: **Copy every digit exactly. Your work depends on it.**

Try this on your next practice test. Small, smart habits become big score boosters.

★ **Be precise. Be powerful.** ★
Tiny care moments make giant score boosts.

Grade 5 Mathematics

Questions: 40 **Duration:** No time limit

Calculator Policy: Calculators are not allowed

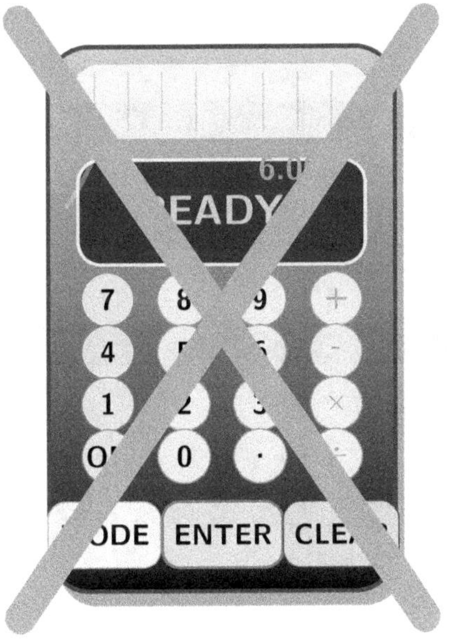

Grade 5 Mathematics Reference Materials

PERIMETER AND AREA

Perimeter of Rectangle	$P = 2l + 2w$ or $P = 2(l + w)$
Area of Rectangle	$A = l \times w$
Area of Triangle	$A = \frac{1}{2} \times b \times h$
Volume of Rectangular Prism	$V = l \times w \times h$

LENGTH

Customary	**Metric**
1 foot (ft) = 12 inches (in.)	1 meter (m) = 100 centimeters (cm)
1 yard (yd) = 3 feet (ft)	1 centimeter (cm) = 10 millimeters (mm)
1 yard (yd) = 36 inches (in.)	1 kilometer (km) = 1,000 meters (m)

CAPACITY

Customary	**Metric**
1 cup (c) = 8 fluid ounces (fl oz)	1 liter (L) = 1,000 milliliters (mL)
1 pint (pt) = 2 cups (c)	
1 quart (qt) = 2 pints (pt)	
1 gallon (gal) = 4 quarts (qt)	

WEIGHT AND MASS

Customary	**Metric**
1 pound (lb) = 16 ounces (oz)	1 kilogram (kg) = 1,000 grams (g)
	1 gram (g) = 1,000 milligrams (mg)

TIME

1 minute (min) = 60 seconds (sec)	1 week = 7 days
1 hour (hr) = 60 minutes (min)	1 year = 12 months
1 day = 24 hours (hr)	1 year = 52 weeks

1) Pattern Iota: 3, 6, 9, 12, 15. Pattern Kappa: 9, 18, 27, 36, 45. Which student correctly identifies the relationship?

- ☐ A. Maria: Kappa is 6 more than Iota
- ☐ B. Leo: Kappa is 3 less than Iota
- ☐ C. Sophie: Kappa is twice Iota, then 3 more
- ☐ D. Juan: Kappa is 3 times Iota

2) A farmer harvests $\frac{3}{5}$ of his wheat crop. The crop weighs 120 pounds. How many pounds did he harvest?

- ☐ A. 36 pounds
- ☐ B. 48 pounds
- ☐ C. 72 pounds
- ☐ D. 80 pounds

3) At a farmers' market, apples cost \$3.29 per lb and oranges cost \$2.74 per lb. If you buy 1 lb of each, what is the total cost?

- ☐ A. \$5.93
- ☐ B. \$6.03
- ☐ C. \$6.13
- ☐ D. \$6.93

4) A soup recipe calls for $\frac{1}{6}$ cup of salt and $\frac{2}{3}$ cup of water. Which amount is more?

Salt Water

$\frac{1}{6}$ $\frac{2}{3}$

- ☐ A. Salt is more
- ☐ B. Cannot determine
- ☐ C. They are equal
- ☐ D. Water is more

5) What is $5 \times \frac{2}{7}$?

☐ A. $\frac{2}{35}$
☐ B. $\frac{10}{7}$
☐ C. $\frac{7}{10}$
☐ D. $\frac{2}{12}$

6) The model shows $\frac{1}{4}$ of a whole split into 4 equal parts. What fraction of the whole is each small part?

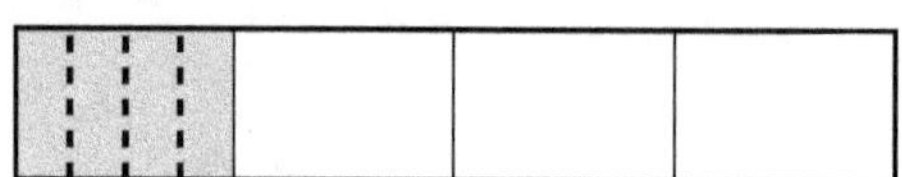

☐ A. $\frac{1}{4}$
☐ B. $\frac{1}{8}$
☐ C. $\frac{1}{16}$
☐ D. $\frac{1}{2}$

7) A landscaper has 6 yards of edging. Each flower bed uses $\frac{1}{4}$ yard of edging. How many flower beds can be edged?

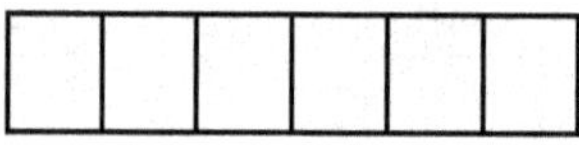

☐ A. 20 beds
☐ B. 36 beds
☐ C. 30 beds
☐ D. 24 beds

8) Sarah has $\frac{3}{4}$ of a pound of chocolate. She uses $\frac{1}{3}$ of it to make brownies. How much chocolate does she use?

☐ A. $\frac{3}{12}$ pounds or $\frac{1}{4}$ pounds
☐ B. $\frac{3}{16}$ pounds
☐ C. $\frac{2}{3}$ pounds
☐ D. 1 pound

9) A student calculates $V = 4 + 3 + 6 = 13$ for dimensions $l = 4$ m, $w = 3$ m, $h = 6$ m. What error was made?

☐ A. She added instead of multiplying.
☐ B. She used the wrong unit.
☐ C. The answer is correct.
☐ D. She divided instead of multiplying.

10) A Venn diagram has circles for quadrilaterals, rectangles, rhombuses, and parallelograms. A square belongs to how many of these circles?

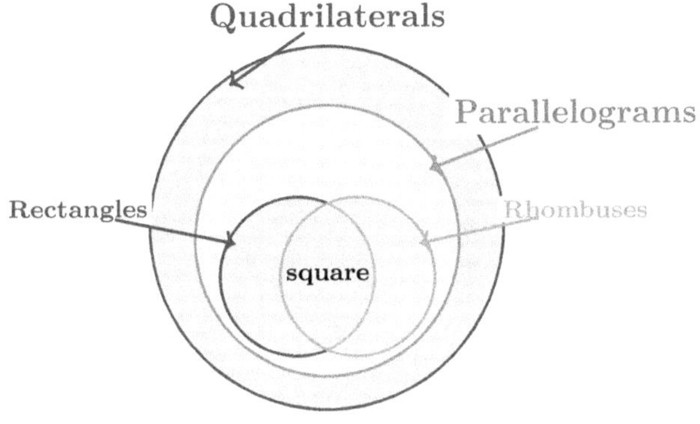

Record your answer in the space provided.

11) If all sides of a parallelogram are equal, what is the most specific name?

☐ A. Quadrilateral
☐ B. Parallelogram
☐ C. Rhombus
☐ D. Rectangle

12) A rectangular prism with dimensions 4 cm × 5 cm × 6 cm is compared to another with dimensions 3 cm × 5 cm × 8 cm. Which statement is true?

Prism	Dimensions
Prism X	4 cm × 5 cm × 6 cm
Prism Y	3 cm × 5 cm × 8 cm

☐ A. Prism X has greater volume

☐ B. Prism Y has greater volume

☐ C. Both have equal volume

☐ D. Cannot determine

13) Point P is shown inside Quadrant I, not on an axis. How many of its coordinates are positive?

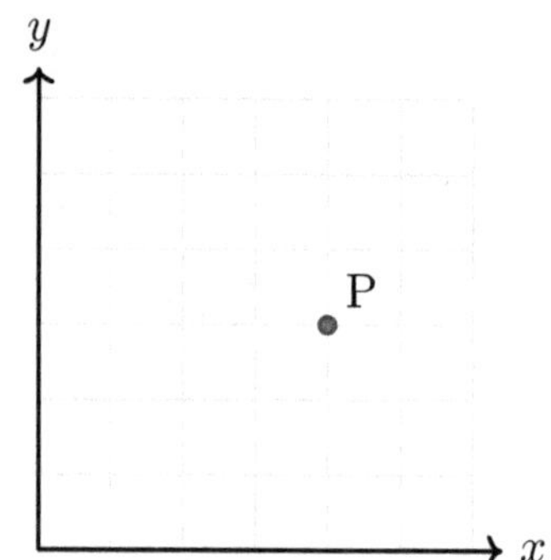

Record your answer in the space provided.

14) Find the product: $80 \times 9{,}000$.

Record your answer in the space provided.

15) Tim had \$50. He spent \$5 on each of 3 items and \$7 for lunch. Which expression represents the money he has left?

☐ A. $50 - [(3 \times 5) + 7]$
☐ B. $(50 - 3) \times (5 + 7)$
☐ C. $50 - (3 + 5 + 7)$
☐ D. $50 - 3 + 5 \times 7$

16) What is 304×2?

☐ A. 600
☐ B. 630
☐ C. 620
☐ D. 608

17) A graph tracks the amount of money saved each week. The point $(7, 35)$ represents how much money was saved after how many weeks?

☐ A. \$7 after 35 weeks
☐ B. \$7 saved after 5 weeks
☐ C. \$42 total
☐ D. \$35 after 7 weeks

18) For the expression $[(8 + 4) \div 2] + 1$, which statements are true? *Select all that apply.*

☐ A. The first step is to add $8 + 4$.
☐ B. The first step is to divide $4 \div 2$.
☐ C. The final value is 7.
☐ D. The final value is 9.

19) What is $\frac{1}{10} \div 3$?

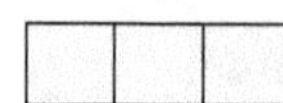

$\frac{1}{10}$ split into 3

☐ A. $\frac{1}{30}$
☐ B. $\frac{3}{10}$
☐ C. $\frac{1}{7}$
☐ D. $\frac{1}{13}$

20) The line plot shows nail lengths (in inches) sorted in a toolbox:

Nail Lengths

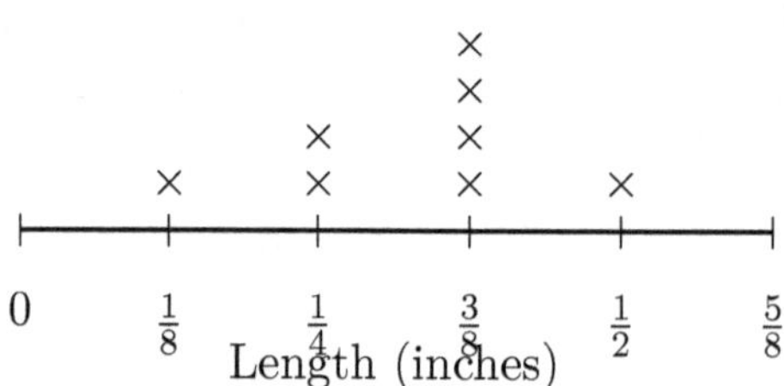

How many nails are $\frac{3}{8}$ inch long?

☐ A. 2
☐ B. 3
☐ C. 4
☐ D. 5

21) A composite play structure is made from two non-overlapping rectangular prisms. Prism A is 5 meters long, 4 meters wide, and 3 meters tall. Prism B is 6 meters long, 2 meters wide, and 5 meters tall. What is the total volume?

☐ A. 60 cubic meters
☐ B. 140 cubic meters
☐ C. 130 cubic meters
☐ D. 120 cubic meters

22) A wall is 30 feet long. A painter covers $\frac{2}{3}$ of it. Does the painter cover more than 30 feet or less than 30 feet?

☐ A. More than 30 feet
☐ B. Less than 30 feet
☐ C. Exactly 30 feet
☐ D. Cannot be determined

23) Which statement is false?

☐ A. $2.3 \times 10 = 23$
☐ B. $2.3 \times 100 = 230$
☐ C. $0.23 \times 100 = 23$
☐ D. $0.023 \times 1000 = 2.3$

24) Express 0.309 in expanded form using fractions.

☐ A. $\frac{3}{10} + \frac{9}{100}$
☐ B. $\frac{3}{100} + \frac{9}{1000}$
☐ C. $\frac{39}{1000}$
☐ D. $\frac{3}{10} + \frac{9}{1000}$

25) Find: $5{,}600 \div 10^2$.

Record your answer in the space provided.

26) Four packages are shipped together. Their weights are: Package 1: 8.5 kg Package 2: 12.3 kg Package 3: 9.7 kg Package 4: 10.5 kg
What is the combined weight in kilograms?

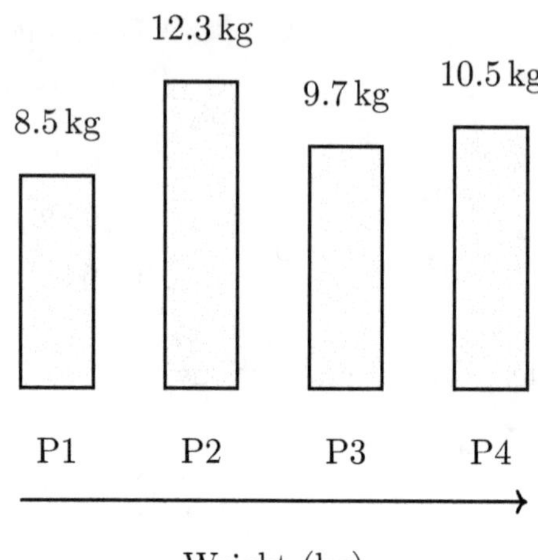

☐ A. 38.5 kg
☐ B. 40.0 kg
☐ C. 41.0 kg
☐ D. 42.5 kg

27) Look at the diagram with labeled angles. Classify by angles.

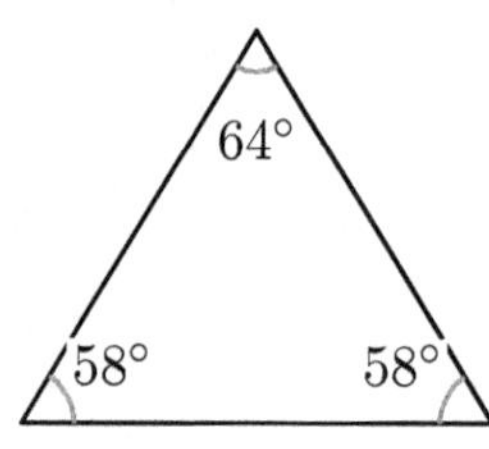

not drawn to scale

☐ A. Right triangle
☐ B. Equiangular triangle
☐ C. Obtuse triangle
☐ D. Acute triangle

28) A baker uses 0.25 kg of sugar in each batch of cookies. How much sugar for 4 batches?

☐ A. 0.4 kg
☐ B. 0.8 kg
☐ C. 1.0 kg
☐ D. 1.2 kg

29) Which ordered pair belongs in the pattern below?

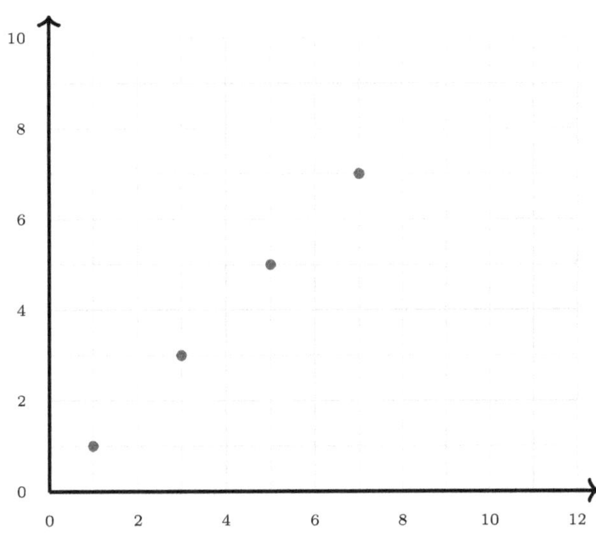

☐ A. (8, 9)
☐ B. (9, 8)
☐ C. (6, 7)
☐ D. (9, 9)

30) A number is represented as $4 + \frac{2}{10} + \frac{5}{100} + \frac{8}{1000}$. What is this number in decimal form?

☐ A. 4.258
☐ B. 4.028
☐ C. 4.852
☐ D. 4.528

31) Multiply: $1\frac{3}{5} \times 2\frac{1}{2}$

	1	$\frac{3}{5}$
2	1×2	$\frac{3}{5} \times 2$
$\frac{1}{2}$	$1 \times \frac{1}{2}$	$\frac{3}{5} \times \frac{1}{2}$

$1\frac{3}{5} \times 2\frac{1}{2}$

☐ A. 4

☐ B. $3\frac{3}{4}$

☐ C. $3\frac{3}{10}$

☐ D. $4\frac{1}{10}$

32) Use the number line below. The dot is at $\frac{2}{3}$. Which fraction with denominator 6 is equivalent to the marked point?

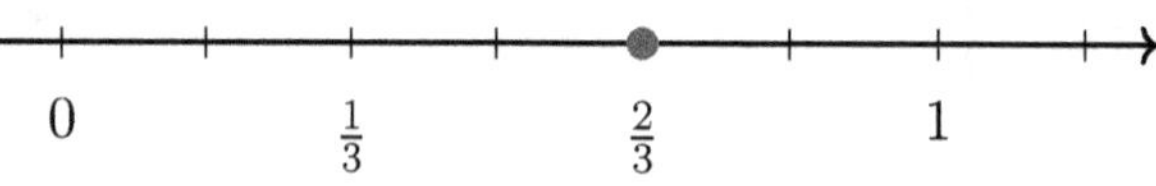

☐ A. $\frac{5}{6}$

☐ B. $\frac{2}{6}$

☐ C. $\frac{3}{6}$

☐ D. $\frac{4}{6}$

33) Convert: 5 pounds = ? ounces.

Record your answer in the space provided.

34) A gardener plants seeds in rows. There are 8 rows with 45 seeds each. How many seeds were planted in total?

☐ A. 320 seeds

☐ B. 340 seeds

☐ C. 360 seeds

☐ D. 380 seeds

35) Pattern: $1, 3, 6, 10, 15, \ldots$ Which statement explains the rule and gives the next two terms?

☐ A. Add 2 each time; next terms are 17 and 19

☐ B. Add 2, then 3, then 4, then 5, and so on; next terms are 21 and 28

☐ C. Multiply by 2; next terms are 30 and 60

☐ D. Add 5 each time; next terms are 20 and 25

36) Without computing, compare: $10 \times \frac{1}{4}$ and $10 \times \frac{1}{2}$

☐ A. $10 \times \frac{1}{4} > 10 \times \frac{1}{2}$

☐ B. $10 \times \frac{1}{4} = 10 \times \frac{1}{2}$

☐ C. $10 \times \frac{1}{4} < 10 \times \frac{1}{2}$

☐ D. They are incomparable

37) What is $12 \div \frac{1}{2}$?

☐ A. 6

☐ B. 12

☐ C. 18

☐ D. 24

38) A point that is 9 units right of the origin and 4 units up from the origin has coordinates:

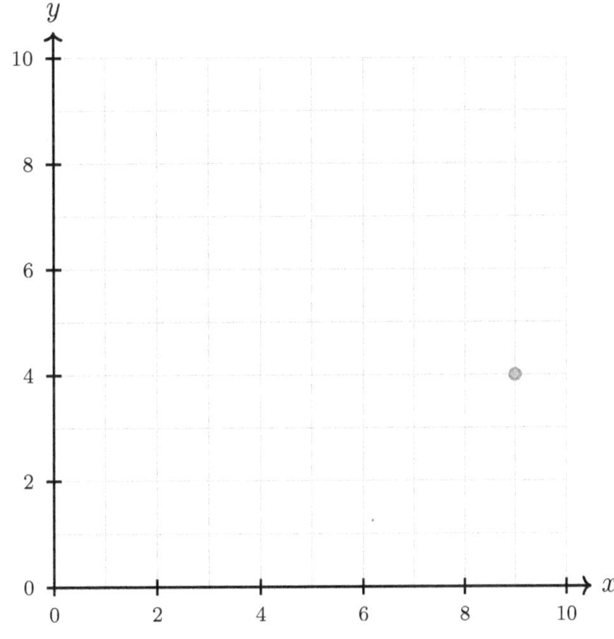

☐ A. $(4, 9)$

☐ B. $(4, 4)$

☐ C. $(9, 9)$

☐ D. $(9, 4)$

39) Maya and Zoe started with one whole sandwich. Maya ate $\frac{3}{8}$ of it, and Zoe ate $\frac{1}{4}$ of it. How much remains?

☐ A. $\frac{3}{8}$
☐ B. $\frac{1}{2}$
☐ C. $\frac{1}{4}$
☐ D. $\frac{5}{8}$

40) Add: $\frac{5}{8} + \frac{1}{6}$

☐ A. $\frac{6}{14}$
☐ B. $\frac{8}{24}$
☐ C. $\frac{6}{8}$
☐ D. $\frac{19}{24}$

End of Practice Test

Take a short breath, then check your work with care. Good corrections can teach almost as much as the test itself.

Plan-First Star!

You finished a full test. That takes focus and stamina.
A short plan saves a long detour.

Plan Before You Solve

Ada Lovelace is often called the first computer programmer. Her superpower? Planning. She wrote down the steps before she ever ran the program.

You can do the same on a math test. Before you compute, write a tiny plan: 1) Find the question. 2) Pick the operation. 3) Check the units.

It feels slow at first, but the plan is the speed. You skip dead ends and head straight for the answer.

Math Mindset Tip: **A 5-second plan saves a 30-second detour.**

First plan, then solve. The plan is the shortcut.
— Math Mindset

Lovelace's Amazing Journey ★

Ada planned because she knew that one missed step could ruin a whole program. The same is true in math.

On a multi-step word problem, missing a step (like a unit conversion or a final addition) costs the whole answer. Planning fixes that.

Try this: before any multi-step problem, write "Step 1, Step 2, Step 3" in the margin. Then solve.

Lovelace's Secret: **Steps in the margin are guardrails for your brain.**

Try this on your next practice test. Small, smart habits become big score boosters.

★ **Plan it. Solve it. Check it.** ★

Small planning, giant payoff.

Grade 5 Math

Grade 5 Mathematics

Questions: 40 **Duration:** No time limit

Calculator Policy: Calculators are not allowed

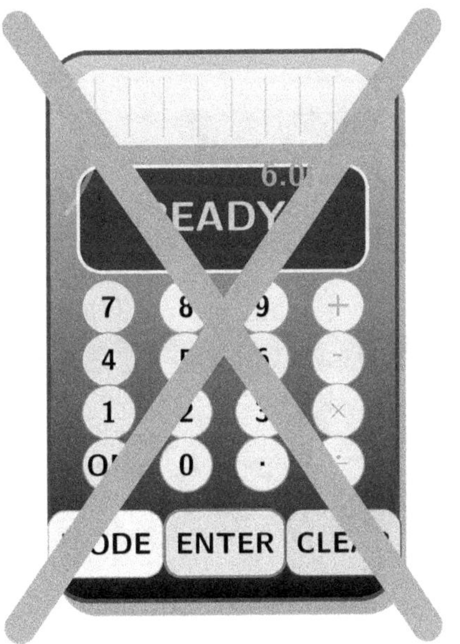

Grade 5 Mathematics Reference Materials

PERIMETER AND AREA

Perimeter of Rectangle	$P = 2l + 2w$ or $P = 2(l + w)$
Area of Rectangle	$A = l \times w$
Area of Triangle	$A = \frac{1}{2} \times b \times h$
Volume of Rectangular Prism	$V = l \times w \times h$

LENGTH

Customary	Metric
1 foot (ft) = 12 inches (in.)	1 meter (m) = 100 centimeters (cm)
1 yard (yd) = 3 feet (ft)	1 centimeter (cm) = 10 millimeters (mm)
1 yard (yd) = 36 inches (in.)	1 kilometer (km) = 1,000 meters (m)

CAPACITY

Customary	Metric
1 cup (c) = 8 fluid ounces (fl oz)	1 liter (L) = 1,000 milliliters (mL)
1 pint (pt) = 2 cups (c)	
1 quart (qt) = 2 pints (pt)	
1 gallon (gal) = 4 quarts (qt)	

WEIGHT AND MASS

Customary	Metric
1 pound (lb) = 16 ounces (oz)	1 kilogram (kg) = 1,000 grams (g)
	1 gram (g) = 1,000 milligrams (mg)

TIME

1 minute (min) = 60 seconds (sec)	1 week = 7 days
1 hour (hr) = 60 minutes (min)	1 year = 12 months
1 day = 24 hours (hr)	1 year = 52 weeks

1) Which figure has volume as an attribute?

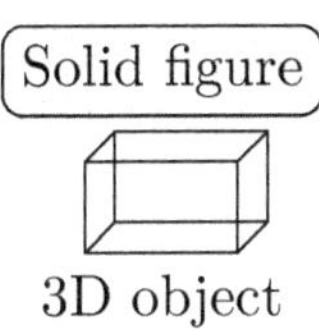

☐ A. A line segment
☐ B. A rectangle
☐ C. A rectangular prism
☐ D. A point

2) Compare: $(20 + 30) \times 7 \square 20 \times 7 + 30 \times 7$

☐ A. >
☐ B. <
☐ C. =
☐ D. Cannot tell

3) A Venn diagram has a large circle for quadrilaterals and a smaller circle inside it for figures with two pairs of parallel sides. A rectangle is placed inside the smaller circle. Why?

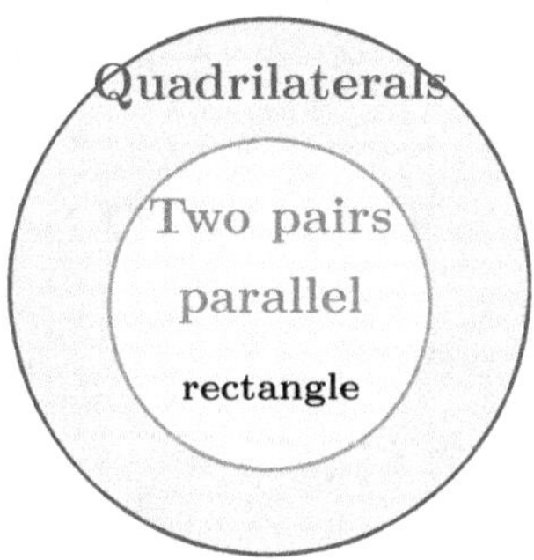

☐ A. It has exactly 3 sides.
☐ B. It is not a polygon.
☐ C. It has no right angles.
☐ D. It has 4 sides and two pairs of parallel sides.

4) A shape is a closed polygon with 5 straight sides and 5 vertices. Which statement correctly describes the shape?

☐ A. It is a pentagon.
☐ B. It is a quadrilateral.
☐ C. It must be a rectangle.
☐ D. It has curved sides.

5) Evaluate: $[5 + (12 \div 4)] \times 2$

☐ A. 14
☐ B. 16
☐ C. 20
☐ D. 22

6) Complete the pattern:

Expression	Value
$3,500 \div 10$	350
$3,500 \div 100$	35
$3,500 \div 1,000$	?

☐ A. 35,000
☐ B. 0.35
☐ C. 350
☐ D. 3.5

7) Which operation changes 2.5 to 250?

☐ A. $\times 10$
☐ B. $\times 100$
☐ C. $\div 10$
☐ D. $\div 100$

8) A piece of fabric is 3 yards long. If you use $\frac{1}{4}$ of it for a project, how many yards do you use?

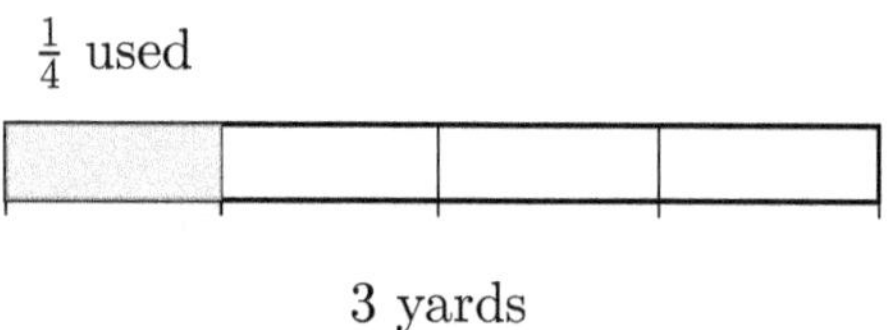

☐ A. $\frac{1}{4}$ yard
☐ B. $\frac{1}{2}$ yard
☐ C. $\frac{3}{4}$ yard
☐ D. 1 yard

9) Two rectangular prisms have the same base (4 by 3 unit cubes), but different heights. Prism A is 2 tall, Prism B is 5 tall. How many more cubes does Prism B hold?

Prism A	Prism B
base 4×3, height 2	base 4×3, height 5

☐ A. 12 unit cubes more

☐ B. 24 unit cubes more

☐ C. 36 unit cubes more

☐ D. 10 unit cubes more

10) A craft project requires $\frac{3}{8}$ meter of ribbon. If you use $\frac{2}{3}$ of that ribbon for the bow, how much ribbon is used for the bow?

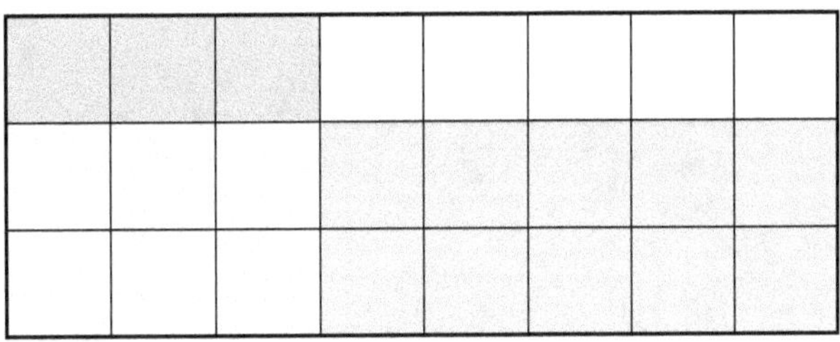

☐ A. $\frac{2}{11}$ meter

☐ B. $\frac{1}{8}$ meter

☐ C. $\frac{3}{10}$ meter

☐ D. $\frac{6}{24}$ meter or $\frac{1}{4}$ meter

11) A tank is $\frac{7}{8}$ full. After using $\frac{3}{8}$ for watering plants, how much remains?

☐ A. $\frac{2}{8}$

☐ B. $\frac{10}{8}$

☐ C. $\frac{5}{8}$

☐ D. $\frac{1}{2}$

12) A rectangle is split into 3 equal columns and 4 equal rows (12 cells total). $\frac{1}{4}$ of the rows and $\frac{2}{3}$ of the columns are shaded. How many cells are shaded?

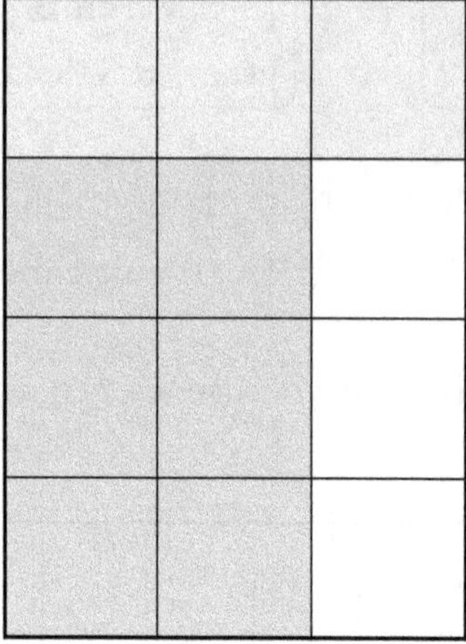

blue: $\frac{2}{3}$ of columns
red: $\frac{1}{4}$ of rows
green: overlap

☐ A. 2 cells
☐ B. 3 cells
☐ C. 4 cells
☐ D. 6 cells

13) Find: 0.082×10^2.

Record your answer in the space provided.

14) Alice brought $1\frac{1}{2}$ lbs grapes, Bob $2\frac{1}{4}$ lbs apples, Chris $\frac{3}{4}$ lb cookies. Total?

☐ A. $4\frac{1}{2}$ lbs
☐ B. $4\frac{1}{4}$ lbs
☐ C. $4\frac{3}{4}$ lbs
☐ D. 5 lbs

15) Carol saw an expression on a sign: $(250 + 75) \times 2$. She reasoned the result must be more than $250 + 75$ but less than what?

☐ A. Less than $250 + 75$
☐ B. Less than $3 \times (250 + 75)$
☐ C. Less than $\frac{1}{2} \times (250 + 75)$
☐ D. Less than $(250 + 75) \div 2$

16) At the start of the day, a thermometer reads 72.45°F. By evening, it drops to 58.13°F. What is the temperature change?

☐ A. 14.32řF
☐ B. 14.58řF
☐ C. 13.58řF
☐ D. 15.42řF

17) Where is the origin on a coordinate grid?

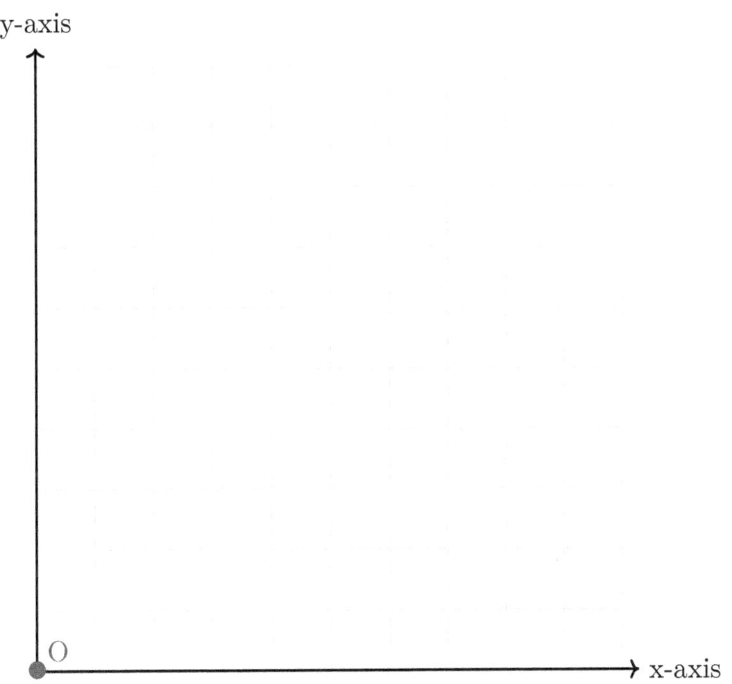

☐ A. In the top right corner
☐ B. On the x-axis only
☐ C. At point $(5, 5)$
☐ D. Where the x-axis and y-axis meet

18) A recipe calls for 2 cups of milk. How many quarts is that? (1 quart = 4 cups)

- ☐ A. $\frac{1}{4}$ quart
- ☐ B. $\frac{1}{2}$ quart
- ☐ C. 1 quart
- ☐ D. 2 quarts

19) A runner estimates her time as 18.75 seconds. What is this rounded to the nearest whole second?

- ☐ A. 18 sec
- ☐ B. 18.7 sec
- ☐ C. 18.8 sec
- ☐ D. 19 sec

20) A school has 15 boxes of science supplies. Each kit uses $\frac{1}{6}$ of a box. How many kits can be made?

- ☐ A. 70 kits
- ☐ B. 80 kits
- ☐ C. 90 kits
- ☐ D. 100 kits

21) Write an expression for: multiply 6 by 10, then divide the result by 2.

Record your expression in the space provided.

22) A box with volume 60 cubic inches has height 5 in. Which pairs of length and width are possible? *Select all that apply.*

- ☐ A. $\ell = 4$, $w = 3$
- ☐ B. $\ell = 6$, $w = 2$
- ☐ C. $\ell = 5$, $w = 3$
- ☐ D. $\ell = 4$, $w = 4$

23) How does dividing by 10^3 affect the decimal point?

☐ A. Moves it 1 place left
☐ B. Moves it 2 places left
☐ C. Moves it 3 places left
☐ D. Moves it 3 places right

24) Pattern: $9 \times 10 = 90$; $9 \times 100 = 900$; $9 \times 1{,}000 = 9{,}000$. How many zeros are in the product $9 \times 1{,}000{,}000$?

☐ A. 4
☐ B. 5
☐ C. 6
☐ D. 7

25) A supply cabinet measures 6 inches long, 7 inches wide, and 5 inches tall. What is its volume?

☐ A. 42 cubic inches
☐ B. 210 cubic inches
☐ C. 30 cubic inches
☐ D. 35 cubic inches

26) Estimate $\frac{1}{10} + \frac{5}{6}$ using 0, $\frac{1}{2}$, and 1 benchmarks.

Record your answer in the space provided.

27) What is $83.5 \div 100$?

☐ A. 0.835
☐ B. 8.35
☐ C. 8,350
☐ D. 0.00835

28) A line plot shows: 2 X's at $\frac{1}{4}$, 4 X's at $\frac{1}{2}$, 1 X at $\frac{3}{4}$. How many measurements total?

Record your answer in the space provided.

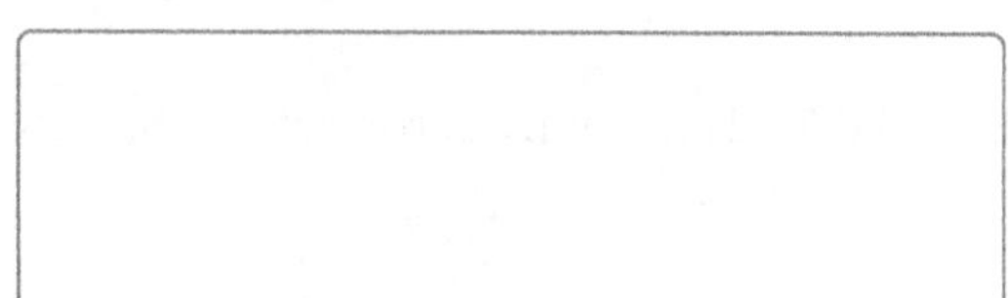

29) One third pound of clay is split equally among 4 students. Which division equation finds each share?

- ☐ A. $4 \div \frac{1}{3} = n$
- ☐ B. $\frac{1}{3} \times 4 = n$
- ☐ C. $\frac{1}{3} \div 4 = n$
- ☐ D. $4 + \frac{1}{3} = n$

30) If you know the volume is 336 cm^3 and two dimensions are 12 cm and 7 cm, what is the third dimension?

- ☐ A. 3 cm
- ☐ B. 6 cm
- ☐ C. 5 cm
- ☐ D. 4 cm

31) The line plot shows pencil lengths, in inches. What is the total length of all 6 pencils?

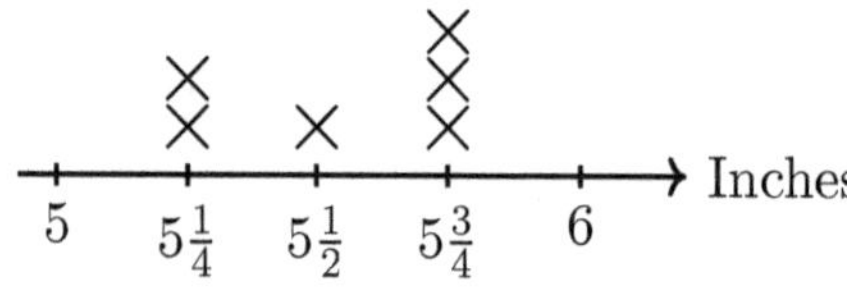

Record your answer in the space provided.

32) Estimate the sum: $3.92 + 4.18$. Which is the best estimate?

☐ A. 7
☐ B. 8
☐ C. 9
☐ D. 10

33) Which number is a common denominator for $\frac{2}{5}$ and $\frac{3}{4}$?

☐ A. 20
☐ B. 9
☐ C. 15
☐ D. 10

34) A weight of 3 kilograms plus 250 grams equals how many grams in total?

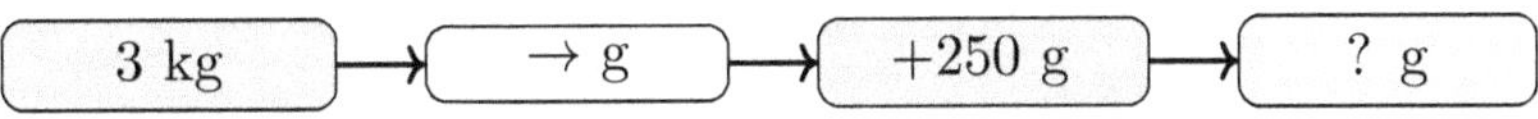

☐ A. 3,250 g
☐ B. 325 g
☐ C. 32,500 g
☐ D. 553 g

35) Subtract and simplify: $10\frac{8}{10} - 6\frac{4}{10}$.

☐ A. $4\frac{2}{5}$
☐ B. $4\frac{3}{10}$
☐ C. $5\frac{1}{5}$
☐ D. $4\frac{1}{5}$

36) What is $23 \times 10 \times 10$?

☐ A. 230
☐ B. 460
☐ C. 23000
☐ D. 2300

37) Two rules create ordered pairs. Rule X doubles the input. Rule Y doubles the input and then adds 1. For input 3, which statement is true?

☐ A. Both rules give the same y value
☐ B. Rule X gives $(3, 6)$ and Rule Y gives $(3, 7)$
☐ C. Rule X gives $(3, 7)$ and Rule Y gives $(3, 6)$
☐ D. Rule Y always has a smaller y than Rule X

38) The model shows 4 wholes, with each whole cut into pieces of size $\frac{1}{4}$. How many pieces of size $\frac{1}{4}$ are there in all?

1 whole

1 whole

1 whole

1 whole

4 wholes, each cut into pieces of size $\frac{1}{4}$

☐ A. 8

☐ B. 16

☐ C. 4

☐ D. 12

39) Which decimal is less than 0.375?

☐ A. 0.38

☐ B. 0.4

☐ C. 0.37

☐ D. 0.375

40) Number line with hops of $\frac{1}{4}$:

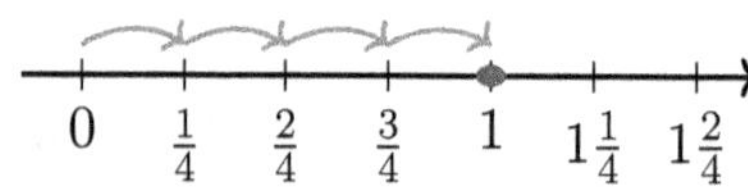

What is $4 \times \frac{1}{4}$?

☐ A. $\frac{3}{4}$

☐ B. 4

☐ C. $\frac{1}{4}$

☐ D. 1

End of Practice Test

Take a short breath, then check your work with care. Good corrections can teach almost as much as the test itself.

Neat Notation Wins! ✓

You finished a full test. That takes focus and stamina.
Clear writing helps your brain see the answer.

Clear Notation Saves Points ★

Gottfried Leibniz invented many of the math symbols you use today, like the ÷ sign and clear ways to write fractions. He believed clear notation makes thinking easier.

Have you ever written a number sloppily, then misread your own "4" as a "9"? That's a notation mistake, not a math mistake. Leibniz would say, "Write so your future-self can read it."

On 5th grade tests, clear digits, neatly stacked numbers, and labeled units (cm, dollars) prevent silly mistakes that cost real points.

Math Mindset Tip: **Write neatly, line up your columns, and label your units. Your eyes will thank you.**

Clear writing is half the answer.
— Math Mindset

Scan me

Leibniz's Amazing Journey ★

Leibniz cared about symbols because symbols carry meaning. A messy "7" that looks like a "1" can ruin a perfect plan.

Try this: when you copy a number, slow down and check that every digit is clear. When you set up multi-digit multiplication, line up your places. When you record an answer, include the unit.

These tiny habits will earn you more points than any new trick.

Leibniz's Secret: Notation is part of math—don't skip it.

Try this on your next practice test. Small, smart habits become big score boosters.

★ Write it clearly. Solve it clearly. ★

Neat notation is silent extra credit.

Grade 5 Math

Grade 5 Mathematics

Questions: 40 **Duration:** No time limit

Calculator Policy: Calculators are not allowed

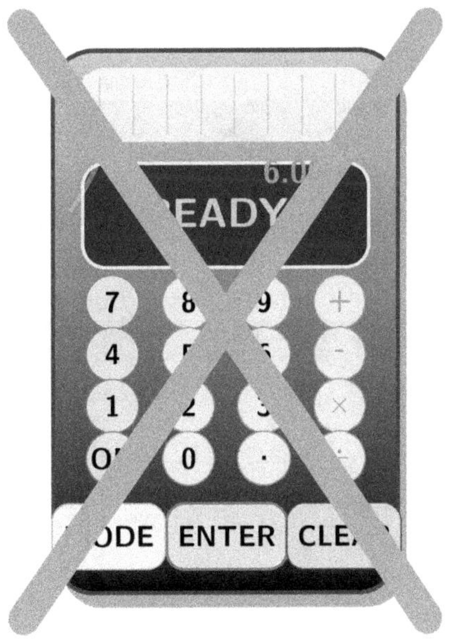

Grade 5 Mathematics Reference Materials

PERIMETER AND AREA

Perimeter of Rectangle	$P = 2l + 2w$ or $P = 2(l + w)$
Area of Rectangle	$A = l \times w$
Area of Triangle	$A = \frac{1}{2} \times b \times h$
Volume of Rectangular Prism	$V = l \times w \times h$

LENGTH

Customary	**Metric**
1 foot (ft) = 12 inches (in.)	1 meter (m) = 100 centimeters (cm)
1 yard (yd) = 3 feet (ft)	1 centimeter (cm) = 10 millimeters (mm)
1 yard (yd) = 36 inches (in.)	1 kilometer (km) = 1,000 meters (m)

CAPACITY

Customary	**Metric**
1 cup (c) = 8 fluid ounces (fl oz)	1 liter (L) = 1,000 milliliters (mL)
1 pint (pt) = 2 cups (c)	
1 quart (qt) = 2 pints (pt)	
1 gallon (gal) = 4 quarts (qt)	

WEIGHT AND MASS

Customary	**Metric**
1 pound (lb) = 16 ounces (oz)	1 kilogram (kg) = 1,000 grams (g)
	1 gram (g) = 1,000 milligrams (mg)

TIME

1 minute (min) = 60 seconds (sec)	1 week = 7 days
1 hour (hr) = 60 minutes (min)	1 year = 12 months
1 day = 24 hours (hr)	1 year = 52 weeks

1) Which statement about $(30 + 20) \div 5$ and $(30 \div 5) + (20 \div 5)$ is correct?

☐ A. First expression is larger
☐ B. Second expression is larger
☐ C. They are equal
☐ D. Cannot be compared

2) What is the missing dimension of this rectangular prism?

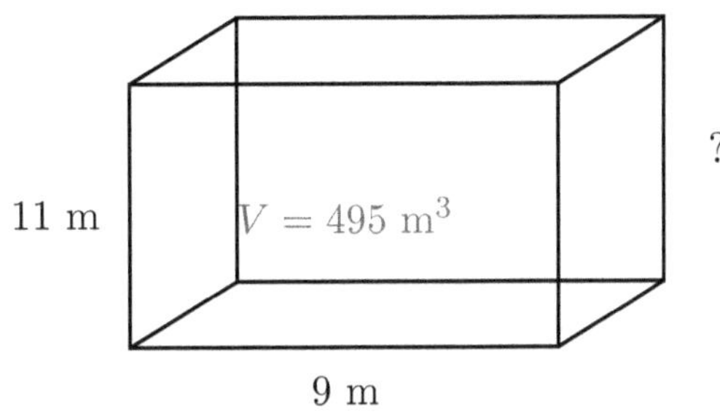

☐ A. 3 m
☐ B. 4 m
☐ C. 5 m
☐ D. 6 m

3) Which name describes a triangle with two equal sides and one right angle?

☐ A. Right isosceles triangle
☐ B. Equilateral triangle
☐ C. Right scalene triangle
☐ D. Obtuse isosceles triangle

4)

Properties Table

Shape	**Parallel sides**	**Must have all sides equal?**	**Must have 90° angles?**
Square	✓	✓	✓
Rectangle	✓	–	✓
Rhombus	✓	✓	–
Trapezoid	at least 1 pair	–	–

A quadrilateral has all four sides equal in length AND all four angles equal to 90°. Using the table, what is the MOST specific name for this shape?

☐ A. Quadrilateral
☐ B. Parallelogram
☐ C. Rectangle
☐ D. Square

5) Write the value of the digit 7 in the number $4.0\underline{7}3$.

Record your answer in the space provided.

6) Reading a coordinate graph, if you can see points at (2, 8), (3, 12), (4, 16), what is the missing y-value for $x = 5$?

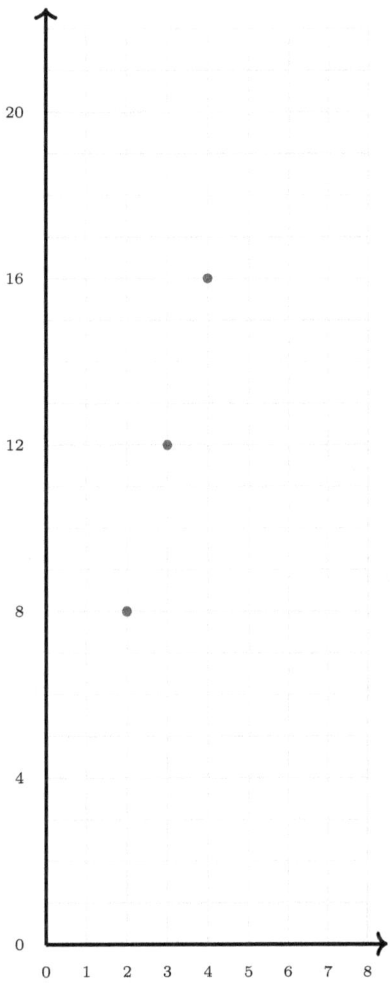

☐ A. 18

☐ B. 20

☐ C. 22

☐ D. 24

7) What is the missing numerator? $\frac{4}{9} = \frac{?}{27}$

☐ A. 8
☐ B. 11
☐ C. 12
☐ D. 16

8) A temperature graph passes through $(0, 50)$ and $(4, 70)$. What is the change in temperature?

Record your answer in the space provided.

9) Pattern P: 2, 4, 6, 8, 10. Pattern Q: 6, 12, 18, 24, 30. What is the rule?

Position	Pattern P	Pattern Q
1	2	6
2	4	12
3	6	18

☐ A. $Q = P + 4$
☐ B. $Q = 3 \times P$
☐ C. $Q = P \times 2 + 2$
☐ D. $Q = P + 2$

10) Ellie packed 4 boxes of pencils with 12 pencils in each box and then gave away 8 pencils. Which expression shows how many pencils she has left?

☐ A. $4 \times (12 - 8)$
☐ B. $(4 \times 12) - 8$
☐ C. $4 + (12 - 8)$
☐ D. $(4 + 12) - 8$

11) Subtract: $\frac{7}{9} - \frac{2}{3}$

☐ A. $\frac{1}{3}$
☐ B. $\frac{5}{9}$
☐ C. $\frac{1}{9}$
☐ D. $\frac{4}{7}$

12) What is 156×6?

☐ A. 900
☐ B. 912
☐ C. 936
☐ D. 948

13) A factory produces 1,200 toys per day. In 15 days, how many toys are produced?

☐ A. 16,000 toys
☐ B. 17,000 toys
☐ C. 18,000 toys
☐ D. 15,000 toys

14) Evan calculates $9 \times \frac{2}{3}$ and gets 18. Is his answer reasonable?

☐ A. Yes, it is reasonable
☐ B. No, it is too large
☐ C. No, it is too small
☐ D. Cannot determine

15) A number line from 0 to $\frac{1}{2}$ is divided into 4 equal segments. What is the length of each segment?

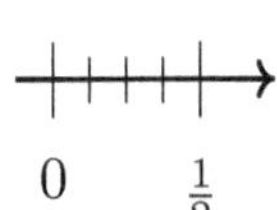

☐ A. $\frac{1}{8}$
☐ B. $\frac{1}{6}$
☐ C. $\frac{1}{4}$
☐ D. $\frac{1}{2}$

16) If a point is moved from $(3, 4)$ to $(7, 4)$, how many units did it move and in which direction?

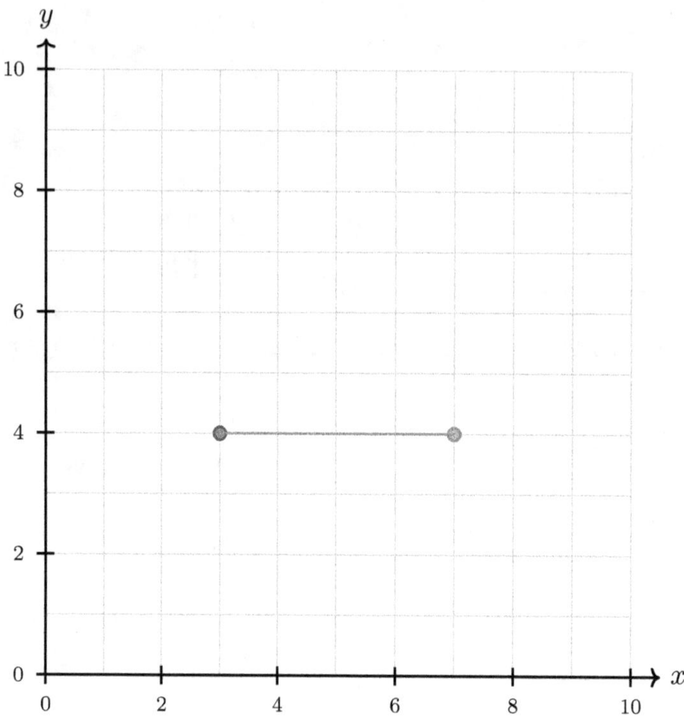

☐ A. 4 units left
☐ B. 4 units down
☐ C. 4 units up
☐ D. 4 units right

17) Write the decimal for "twelve and nine thousandths".

Record your answer in the space provided.

18) A farmer ships 2,904 pounds of apples in crates that hold 44 pounds each. How many crates are filled?

2,904 pounds

$\div$ 44 pounds per crate
= ? crates

☐ A. 64
☐ B. 66
☐ C. 68
☐ D. 70

19) What is $6.3 \div 3$?

☐ A. 1.8
☐ B. 2.0
☐ C. 2.1
☐ D. 9.0

20)

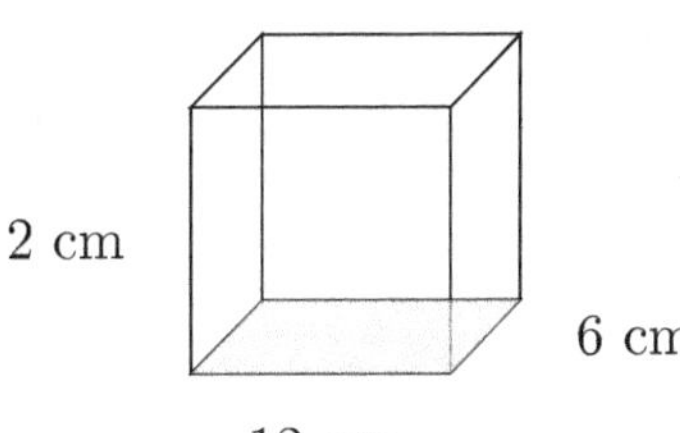

12 cm

A rectangular prism has dimensions shown. What is the volume?

☐ A. 20 cm^3
☐ B. 72 cm^3
☐ C. 36 cm^3
☐ D. 144 cm^3

21) Which statements about $\frac{2}{5} + \frac{1}{4}$ are true? *Select all that apply.*

☐ A. A common denominator is 20.
☐ B. The sum is $\frac{13}{20}$.
☐ C. The sum is $\frac{3}{9}$.
☐ D. A common denominator is 9.

22) Look at the pattern: $2, 20, 200, 2{,}000, \ldots$ What is the next number?

☐ A. 2,002
☐ C. 200,000
☐ B. 2,000,000
☐ D. 20,000

23) A box of crayons has 36 crayons. If you use $\frac{2}{9}$ of them for a project, how many do you use?

☐ A. 4 crayons
☐ C. 18 crayons
☐ B. 8 crayons
☐ D. 28 crayons

24) A composite museum stand is made from two non-overlapping rectangular prisms. Prism A is 7 inches long, 4 inches wide, and 6 inches tall. Prism B is 6 inches long, 4 inches wide, and 2 inches tall. What is the total volume?

☐ A. 168 cubic inches
☐ C. 48 cubic inches
☐ B. 244 cubic inches
☐ D. 216 cubic inches

25) A storage room is 18 feet long, 12 feet wide, and 10 feet tall. If identical boxes each occupy 360 cubic feet and exactly fill the room with no gaps or overlaps, how many boxes fit in the storage room?

☐ A. 4 boxes
☐ C. 8 boxes
☐ B. 6 boxes
☐ D. 10 boxes

26) A baker uses $2\frac{1}{4}$ pounds of sugar per batch of cookies. If she makes 4 batches, how many pounds of sugar does she use?

☐ A. 10
☐ C. 8
☐ B. $8\frac{1}{2}$
☐ D. 9

27) Find: $6 \div \frac{1}{3}$.

Record your answer in the space provided.

28) Without calculating, compare: $(55 + 17) \times 6 \square (55 + 17)$

☐ A. Cannot tell

☐ B. $<$

☐ C. $=$

☐ D. $>$

29) Estimate: $\frac{4}{9} + \frac{1}{12}$. Which benchmark is the best estimate?

☐ A. 0

☐ B. $\frac{1}{2}$

☐ C. 1

☐ D. 2

30) A bag holds 2 kg 400 g. How many grams is that?

Record your answer in the space provided.

31) The line plot shows the lengths, in feet, of boards used for a project:

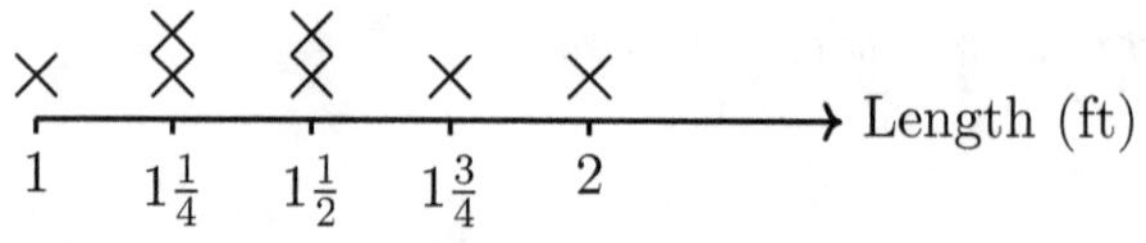

× ×× ×× × ×

1 $1\frac{1}{4}$ $1\frac{1}{2}$ $1\frac{3}{4}$ 2 → Length (ft)

What is the total length of all the boards?

☐ A. 8 feet

☐ B. $11\frac{1}{2}$ feet

☐ C. 10 feet

☐ D. $9\frac{1}{4}$ feet

32) Which phrase represents $5 + 2 \times 6$?

☐ A. Five more than the product of 2 and 6

☐ B. The product of 5, 2, and 6

☐ C. 2 less than the sum of 5 and 6

☐ D. 6 times the sum of 5 and 2

33) A Venn diagram has circles for "4 equal sides" and "4 right angles." A rhombus that is not a square belongs where?

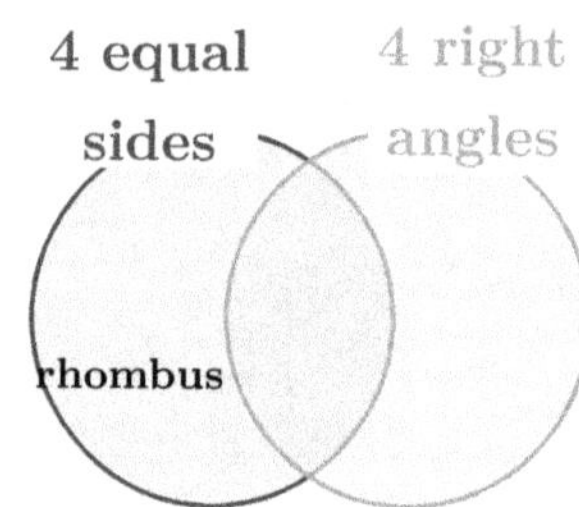

☐ A. In "4 right angles" only

☐ B. In the intersection

☐ C. In "4 equal sides" only

☐ D. Outside both circles

34) The area model shown represents $\frac{1}{5} \times \frac{3}{4}$.

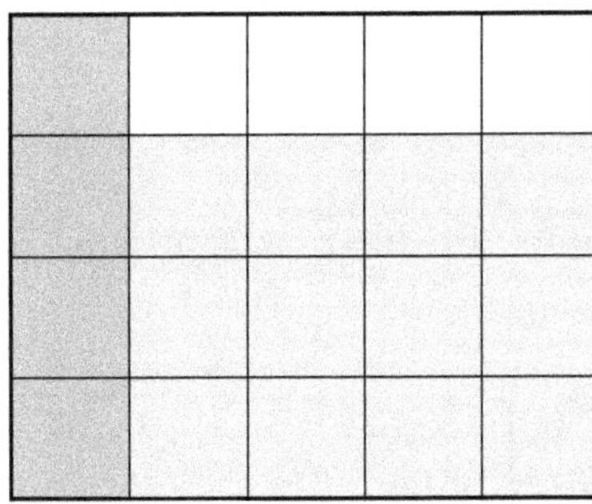

What is the product?

☐ A. $\frac{1}{9}$
☐ B. $\frac{3}{20}$
☐ C. $\frac{1}{5}$
☐ D. $\frac{3}{5}$

35) This shape has 2 congruent sides and 1 right angle. What is it?

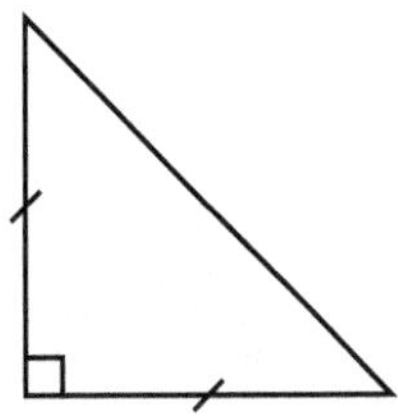

☐ A. Scalene triangle
☐ B. Isosceles right triangle
☐ C. Equilateral triangle
☐ D. Obtuse triangle

36) A furniture store has 5 yards of fabric. Each chair cushion needs $\frac{1}{6}$ yard. How many cushions can be covered?

Each yard is divided into sixth-yard lengths

5 yards shown

☐ A. 24 cushions
☐ B. 28 cushions
☐ C. 30 cushions
☐ D. 32 cushions

37) What is $9,200 \div 1,000$?

☐ A. 92,000
☐ B. 92
☐ C. 920
☐ D. 9.2

38) A construction project requires a cable that is at least 8,500 millimeters long. Which cable meets the requirement?

Cable A	Cable B	Cable C	Cable D
8.4 m	8.7 m	8,200 mm	0.82 km

☐ A. Cable A only
☐ B. Cables A and C only
☐ C. Cables B and D only
☐ D. Cables A, B, and D only

39) What is 0.45×100?

☐ A. 4.5
☐ B. 450
☐ C. 4500
☐ D. 45

40) Simplify then multiply: $\frac{4}{10} \times \frac{5}{8}$. What is the final answer in simplest form?

☐ A. $\frac{20}{80}$
☐ B. $\frac{3}{8}$
☐ C. $\frac{1}{2}$
☐ D. $\frac{1}{4}$

End of Practice Test

Take a short breath, then check your work with care. Good corrections can teach almost as much as the test itself.

Sketch It Out! ✓

You finished a full test. That takes focus and stamina.

Pictures unlock answers that words hide.

Draw the Problem ★

Maryam Mirzakhani was the first woman to win the Fields Medal, the top math prize. She loved drawing as much as solving. Her notebooks were full of doodles, diagrams, and shapes.

She said her drawings helped her see the math. When numbers were hard, pictures made them easier.

In 5th grade, this works for area, perimeter, fractions, time, and word problems. Sketch it, and the answer often shows up.

Math Mindset Tip: **When stuck, draw. A small sketch reveals the path forward.**

A picture is your shortcut to understanding.

— Math Mindset

Mirzakhani's Amazing Journey ★

Maryam's drawings weren't fancy. They were simple shapes labeled with numbers and arrows.

Try this: on the next word problem, draw a quick picture in the margin. A bar, a number line, a rectangle, a circle. Label what you know.

When the picture is clear, the math becomes clear too.

Mirzakhani's Secret: **Math is visual—draw it and you'll see it.**

Try this on your next practice test. Small, smart habits become big score boosters.

★ Sketch. Label. Solve. ★

Your drawing is your guide to the answer.

Grade 5 Mathematics

Questions: 40 **Duration:** No time limit

Calculator Policy: Calculators are not allowed

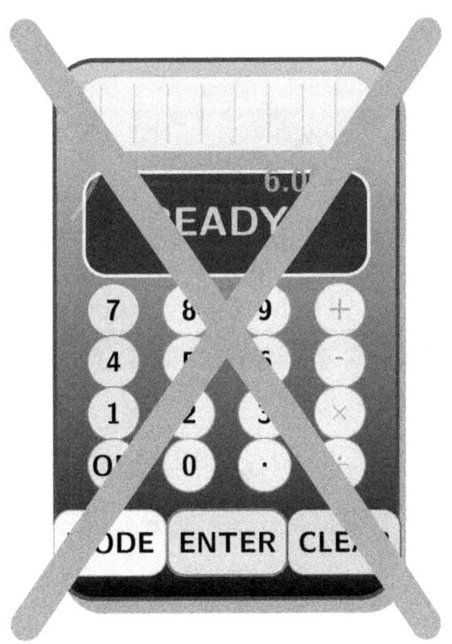

Grade 5 Mathematics Reference Materials

PERIMETER AND AREA

Perimeter of Rectangle	$P = 2l + 2w$ or $P = 2(l + w)$
Area of Rectangle	$A = l \times w$
Area of Triangle	$A = \frac{1}{2} \times b \times h$
Volume of Rectangular Prism	$V = l \times w \times h$

LENGTH

Customary	**Metric**
1 foot (ft) = 12 inches (in.)	1 meter (m) = 100 centimeters (cm)
1 yard (yd) = 3 feet (ft)	1 centimeter (cm) = 10 millimeters (mm)
1 yard (yd) = 36 inches (in.)	1 kilometer (km) = 1,000 meters (m)

CAPACITY

Customary	**Metric**
1 cup (c) = 8 fluid ounces (fl oz)	1 liter (L) = 1,000 milliliters (mL)
1 pint (pt) = 2 cups (c)	
1 quart (qt) = 2 pints (pt)	
1 gallon (gal) = 4 quarts (qt)	

WEIGHT AND MASS

Customary	**Metric**
1 pound (lb) = 16 ounces (oz)	1 kilogram (kg) = 1,000 grams (g)
	1 gram (g) = 1,000 milligrams (mg)

TIME

1 minute (min) = 60 seconds (sec)	1 week = 7 days
1 hour (hr) = 60 minutes (min)	1 year = 12 months
1 day = 24 hours (hr)	1 year = 52 weeks

1) The first input is 1 and the first output is 1. The output doubles each time. Give ordered pairs (input, output) for inputs 1, 2, 3, and 4.

☐ A. $(1,2),(2,4),(3,6),(4,8)$
☐ B. $(1,1),(2,2),(3,4),(4,8)$
☐ C. $(1,2),(2,4),(3,8),(4,16)$
☐ D. $(1,1),(2,3),(3,5),(4,7)$

2) A garden project requires 1.45 m of wood trim and 2.38 m of border. How much material is needed total?

☐ A. 3.73 m
☐ B. 4.83 m
☐ C. 3.93 m
☐ D. 3.83 m

3) A recipe calls for $1\frac{1}{2}$ cups of flour. If you make $\frac{2}{3}$ of the recipe, how much flour do you need?

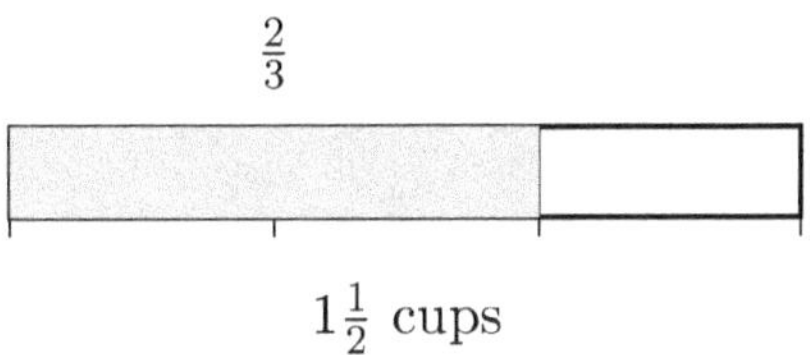

☐ A. $\frac{2}{3}$ cup
☐ B. $1\frac{1}{2}$ cups
☐ C. $1\frac{1}{3}$ cups
☐ D. 1 cup

4)

Expression	**Value**
$29.7 \div 10 = ?$	

☐ A. 29.7
☐ B. 297
☐ C. 2.97
☐ D. 0.297

5) Write the expanded form of 2.34 using place values.

☐ A. $2 + 3 + 4$
☐ B. $20 + 30 + 4$
☐ C. $2 + 0.03 + 0.4$
☐ D. $2 + 0.3 + 0.04$

6) Which arrow correctly shows 0.7×100?

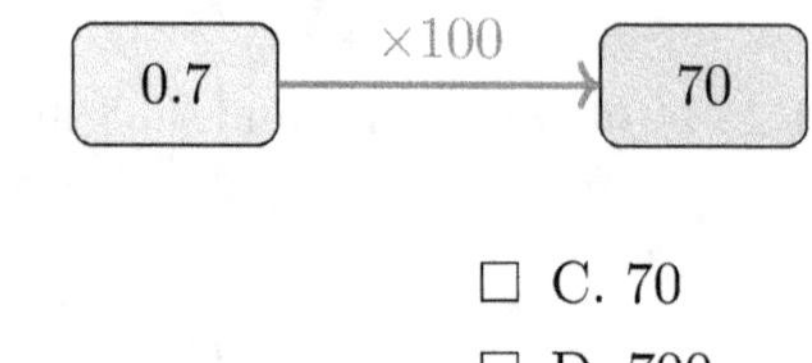

☐ A. 0.007
☐ B. 7
☐ C. 70
☐ D. 700

7) A box is 7 cubes long, 2 cubes wide, and 3 cubes tall. What is its volume in cubic units?

Record your answer in the space provided.

8) Evaluate the expression: $48 \div (6 + 2) + 5 \times 3$

Record your answer in the space provided.

9) A runner training for a race completed 8.75 miles. She plans to run 12.5 miles. How many miles are left?

☐ A. 3.85 miles
☐ B. 3.95 miles
☐ C. 4.15 miles
☐ D. 3.75 miles

10) Number line showing three points. Use the plotted decimals to answer.

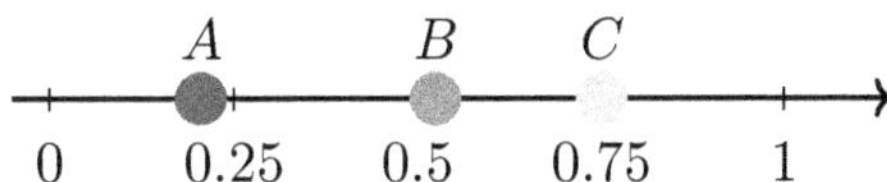

If point A is 0.205, point B is 0.525, point C is 0.75, which is closest to 0.5?

☐ A. Point A
☐ B. Point B
☐ C. Point C
☐ D. Cannot tell

11) Which division equation tells how many $\frac{1}{5}$ parts are in 1 whole?

☐ A. $1 \div \frac{1}{5} = 5$
☐ B. $5 \div \frac{1}{5} = 25$
☐ C. $\frac{1}{5} \div 5 = \frac{1}{25}$
☐ D. $5 + \frac{1}{5} = 5.2$

12) A prism has volume 200 m^3, length 8 m, and width 5 m. Find its height.

Record your answer in the space provided.

13) A ribbon is $7\frac{1}{2}$ meters long. Emma cuts off $3\frac{1}{2}$ meters. How much ribbon is left?

☐ A. $3\frac{1}{2}$ m
☐ B. 4 m
☐ C. $4\frac{1}{2}$ m
☐ D. 5 m

14) A store plots sales data where the x-axis is "Units Sold" and the y-axis is "Revenue in Dollars." What does point $(40, 200)$ tell us about the sale?

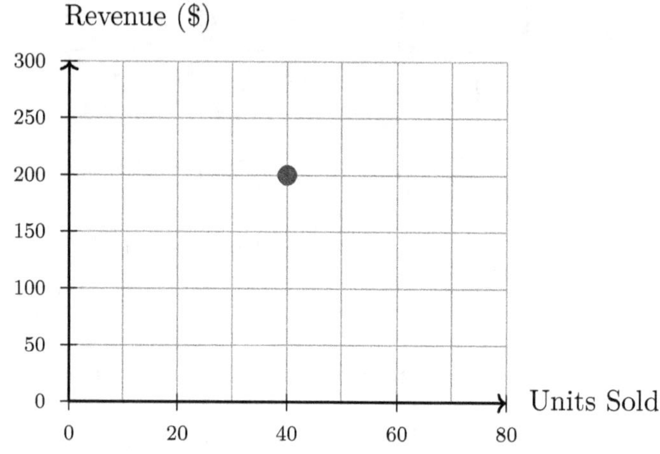

☐ A. 40 units sold for $40
☐ B. 40 units sold for $200
☐ C. 240 units sold in total
☐ D. 200 units sold for $40

15) Which set of equivalent fractions shows $\frac{5}{6}$ and $\frac{3}{8}$ rewritten with LCD 24?

☐ A. $\frac{15}{24}$ and $\frac{9}{24}$
☐ B. $\frac{20}{24}$ and $\frac{12}{24}$
☐ C. $\frac{20}{24}$ and $\frac{9}{24}$
☐ D. $\frac{15}{24}$ and $\frac{12}{24}$

16) Which pair has two expressions that both equal 5000?

☐ A. 40×10 and 4×100
☐ B. 40×10 and 4×1000
☐ C. 50×100 and 500×10
☐ D. 30×1000 and 3×10000

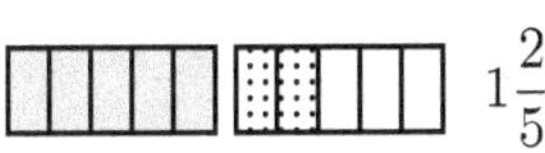

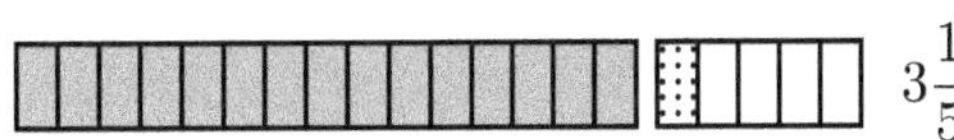

17)

Add: $1\frac{2}{5} + 3\frac{1}{5}$

☐ A. $4\frac{2}{5}$
☐ B. $4\frac{3}{5}$
☐ C. 5
☐ D. $4\frac{1}{5}$

18) Which long-division statements are true for $845 \div 13$? *Select all that apply.*

☐ A. The quotient is 65.
☐ B. There is no remainder.
☐ C. The quotient is 63.
☐ D. There is a remainder of 5.

19) A fence is 72 feet long. Posts are placed every 8 feet. How many posts are needed if posts go at the beginning and end?

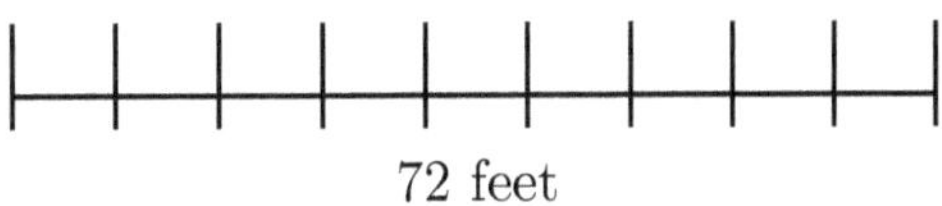

72 feet

☐ A. 9 posts
☐ B. 8 posts
☐ C. 10 posts
☐ D. 11 posts

20) The model shows 1 whole cut into pieces of size $\frac{1}{2}$. How many pieces of size $\frac{1}{2}$ are there in all?

1 whole

1 whole cut into pieces of size $\frac{1}{2}$

☐ A. 3
☐ B. 1
☐ C. 2
☐ D. 4

21) Which two points have the same y-coordinate?

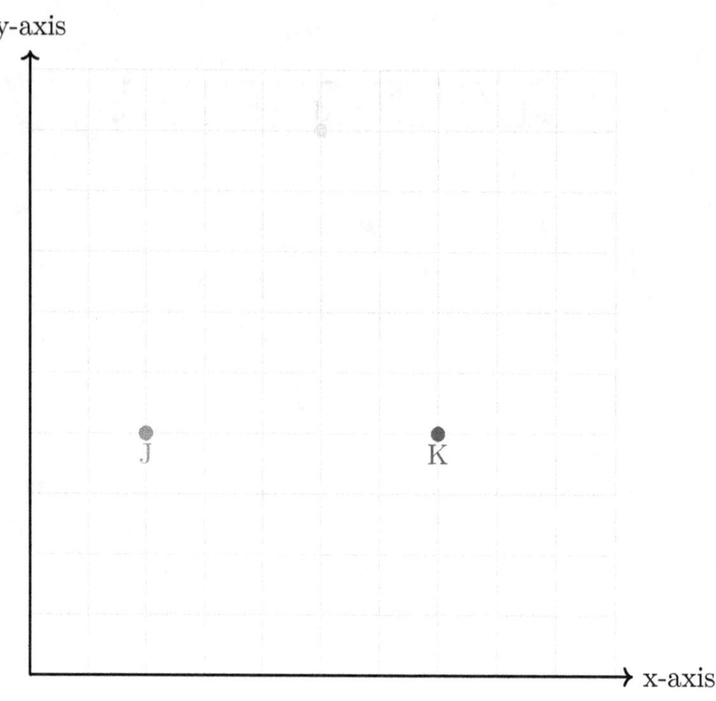

☐ A. J and K
☐ B. J and L
☐ C. K and L
☐ D. All three

22) Add: $\frac{4}{9} + \frac{1}{3}$

☐ A. $\frac{5}{12}$
☐ B. $\frac{7}{9}$
☐ C. $\frac{5}{9}$
☐ D. $\frac{4}{9}$

23) Error analysis: Two students round 11.348 to the nearest tenth. Maya gets 11.3, Jamal gets 11.4. Who is correct?

☐ A. Neither is correct
☐ B. Jamal is correct
☐ C. Both are correct
☐ D. Maya is correct

24) A ribbon is 2 yards long. Use the bar model to find the length in feet.

Yard 1	Yard 2

1 ft	1 ft	1 ft	1 ft	1 ft	1 ft

☐ A. 6 feet ☐ C. 8 feet

☐ B. 5 feet ☐ D. 4 feet

25) Five wholes are divided into pieces of size $\frac{1}{3}$. Which equation finds how many one-third pieces there are?

☐ A. $\frac{1}{3} \div 5 = n$ ☐ C. $5 + \frac{1}{3} = n$

☐ B. $5 \times \frac{1}{3} = n$ ☐ D. $5 \div \frac{1}{3} = n$

26) How many zeros are in the product $2{,}000 \times 50$?

☐ A. 3 ☐ C. 5

☐ B. 4 ☐ D. 6

27) What is $\frac{7}{8} \times 2$?

☐ A. $\frac{7}{16}$ ☐ C. $\frac{7}{10}$

☐ B. $\frac{2}{8}$ ☐ D. $1\frac{3}{4}$

28) A baker removes $\frac{1}{5}$ cup for one recipe and $\frac{2}{7}$ cup for another from 1-cup measure. Remaining?

☐ A. $\frac{18}{35}$ cup ☐ C. $\frac{24}{35}$ cup

☐ B. $\frac{3}{12}$ cup ☐ D. $\frac{1}{35}$ cup

29) How many times greater is the digit 6 in the tenths place compared to the digit 6 in the hundredths place?

☐ A. 2 times ☐ C. 10 times

☐ B. 5 times ☐ D. 100 times

30) A classroom model measures 6 feet long, 7 feet wide, and 8 feet tall. What is its volume?

☐ A. 42 cubic feet
☐ B. 48 cubic feet
☐ C. 336 cubic feet
☐ D. 56 cubic feet

31) The line plot shows the heights of plants in Mrs. Garcia's garden:

Plant Heights in Garden

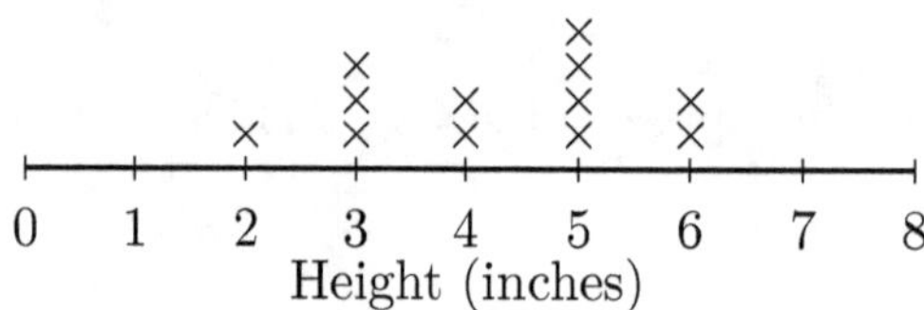

What is the most common plant height?

☐ A. 3 inches
☐ B. 4 inches
☐ C. 5 inches
☐ D. 6 inches

32) A rectangular prism is built from unit cubes arranged in 3 layers. Each layer has 4 rows and 5 columns of cubes. How many unit cubes are in the entire prism?

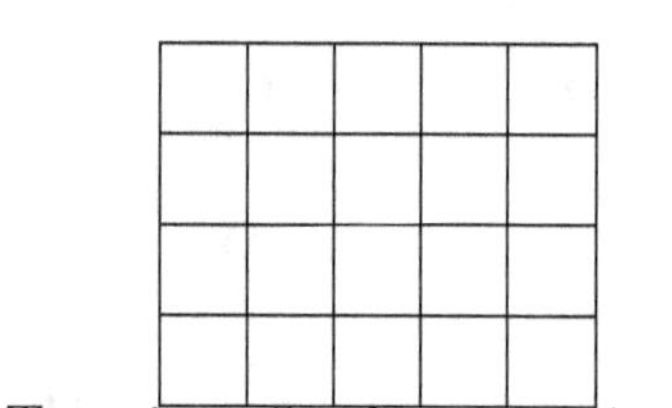

Top view: 5 columns × 4 rows

3 layers

☐ A. 12
☐ B. 20
☐ C. 60
☐ D. 80

33) Find: 0.4×0.6.

Record your answer in the space provided.

34) Which rectangular prism has a volume of 84 cm^3?

A	B	C	D
$4 \times 3 \times 6$ cm	$6 \times 2 \times 7$ cm	$5 \times 3 \times 6$ cm	$4 \times 5 \times 4$ cm

☐ A. First prism
☐ B. Second prism
☐ C. Third prism
☐ D. Fourth prism

35) Multiply: $4\frac{1}{3} \times 1\frac{1}{2}$

☐ A. $5\frac{5}{6}$
☐ B. $7\frac{1}{3}$
☐ C. $4\frac{1}{3}$
☐ D. $6\frac{1}{2}$

36) Coordinate Pattern:

x	y
1	2
2	5
3	8
4	11

Which rule describes the relationship?

☐ A. Multiply the input by 3, then subtract 1
☐ B. Add 1 to the input
☐ C. Double the input, then add 1
☐ D. Multiply the input by 4, then subtract 2

37) Nora starts at (1, 2). She adds 2 to the x-coordinate and 3 to the y-coordinate to get her next point. If she continues this pattern, what will be her fourth point?

☐ A. (8, 14)
☐ B. (6, 10)
☐ C. (7, 11)
☐ D. (5, 8)

38) Find 7×10^2.

Record your answer in the space provided.

39) Two number sequences are shown. Sequence 1: 5, 10, 15, 20, 25. Sequence 2: 1, 2, 3, 4, 5. Write the rule for Sequence 2 in terms of Sequence 1.

Sequence 1	Sequence 2
5	1
10	2
15	3
20	4

☐ A. Sequence 2 = Sequence 1 $\div 5$
☐ B. Sequence 2 = Sequence 1 -4
☐ C. Sequence 2 = Sequence 1 $\times 5$
☐ D. Sequence 2 = Sequence 1 $+1$

40) Which figure is described as having exactly one pair of parallel sides and is not a parallelogram?

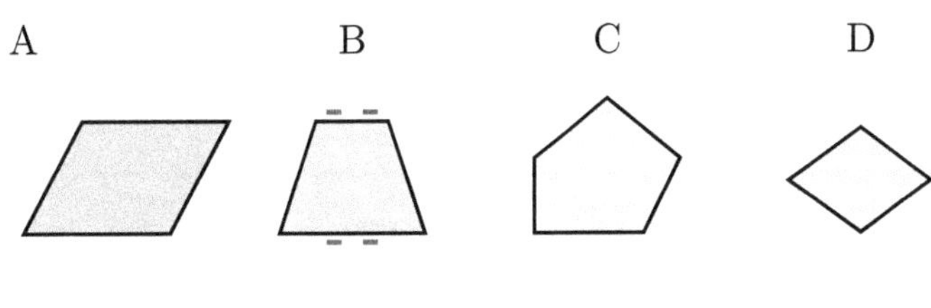

☐ A. Figure A
☐ B. Figure B
☐ C. Figure C
☐ D. Figure D

End of Practice Test

Take a short breath, then check your work with care. Good corrections can teach almost as much as the test itself.

Math Teamwork! ✓

You finished a full test. That takes focus and stamina.

Talking through math makes thinking sharper.

Share Ideas, Learn Faster ★

Akio loved math, but his favorite part was talking about it. When a problem stumped him, he explained it out loud to his little sister, his stuffed bear, or even his pencil.

Saying the problem out loud forced him to slow down. Often, the answer appeared while he was still talking.

On a test, you can't talk out loud, but you can "talk" in your head. Read the problem to yourself in your own words. Then solve.

Math Mindset Tip: **Explain a problem to yourself first. Your words are your map.**

If you can explain it, you can solve it.

— Math Mindset

Akio's Amazing Journey ★

Akio noticed that hearing his own voice unstuck his brain. He stopped worrying about "sounding smart" and started just thinking out loud.

On a tricky test problem, ask yourself silently: "What is this asking? What do I know? What's missing?" Answer in your own words. The answer often appears.

It works because explaining is thinking. The clearer you explain, the clearer you think.

Akio's Secret: **Explain first. Solve second.**

Try this on your next practice test. Small, smart habits become big score boosters.

★ Talk it through. Then solve it through. ★

Your own words are your best math tool.

Grade 5 Math

Grade 5 Mathematics

Questions: 40 **Duration:** No time limit

Calculator Policy: Calculators are not allowed

Grade 5 Mathematics Reference Materials

PERIMETER AND AREA

Perimeter of Rectangle	$P = 2l + 2w$ or $P = 2(l + w)$
Area of Rectangle	$A = l \times w$
Area of Triangle	$A = \frac{1}{2} \times b \times h$
Volume of Rectangular Prism	$V = l \times w \times h$

LENGTH

Customary	Metric
1 foot (ft) = 12 inches (in.)	1 meter (m) = 100 centimeters (cm)
1 yard (yd) = 3 feet (ft)	1 centimeter (cm) = 10 millimeters (mm)
1 yard (yd) = 36 inches (in.)	1 kilometer (km) = 1,000 meters (m)

CAPACITY

Customary	Metric
1 cup (c) = 8 fluid ounces (fl oz)	1 liter (L) = 1,000 milliliters (mL)
1 pint (pt) = 2 cups (c)	
1 quart (qt) = 2 pints (pt)	
1 gallon (gal) = 4 quarts (qt)	

WEIGHT AND MASS

Customary	Metric
1 pound (lb) = 16 ounces (oz)	1 kilogram (kg) = 1,000 grams (g)
	1 gram (g) = 1,000 milligrams (mg)

TIME

1 minute (min) = 60 seconds (sec)	1 week = 7 days
1 hour (hr) = 60 minutes (min)	1 year = 12 months
1 day = 24 hours (hr)	1 year = 52 weeks

1) Which expression equals 6?

☐ A. $600 \div 100$
☐ B. $600 \div 10$
☐ C. $60 \div 100$
☐ D. $6 \div 100$

2) Four points are plotted to form a quadrilateral: $(1, 2)$, $(7, 2)$, $(7, 6)$, and $(1, 6)$. What shape is formed?

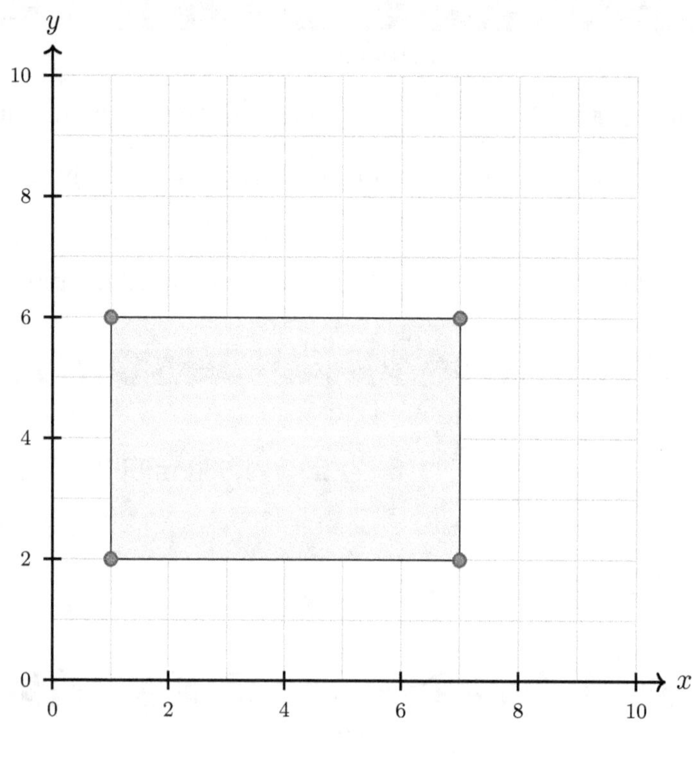

☐ A. Trapezoid
☐ B. Triangle
☐ C. Rectangle
☐ D. Hexagon

3) A composite museum stand is made from two non-overlapping rectangular prisms. Prism A is 5 inches long, 4 inches wide, and 6 inches tall. Prism B is 6 inches long, 4 inches wide, and 2 inches tall. What is the total volume?

☐ A. 120 cubic inches
☐ B. 168 cubic inches
☐ C. 48 cubic inches
☐ D. 188 cubic inches

4) A concert hall has 39 sections with 28 seats in each section. How many seats are in the concert hall?

☐ A. 1,080
☐ B. 1,110
☐ C. 1,100
☐ D. 1,092

5) A clothing store has $\frac{4}{8}$ of its inventory on sale. What is this fraction in simplest form?

☐ A. $\frac{1}{8}$
☐ B. $\frac{2}{8}$
☐ C. $\frac{1}{2}$
☐ D. $\frac{3}{8}$

6) The matching tick marks show all three sides are equal. Looking at the diagram, identify the triangle type based on both sides and angles.

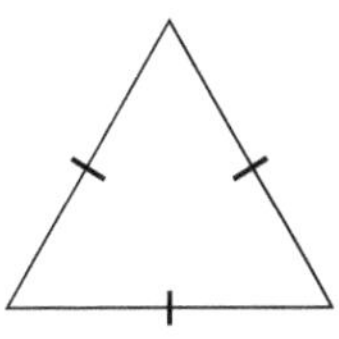

☐ A. Scalene acute
☐ B. Isosceles acute
☐ C. Equilateral acute
☐ D. Right isosceles

7) A pizza is cut into 8 slices. You eat $\frac{3}{8}$ of the pizza. How many slices do you eat?

☐ A. 1 slice
☐ B. 2 slices
☐ C. 4 slices
☐ D. 3 slices

8) Tommy has $\frac{3}{4}$ gallon milk. Uses $\frac{1}{3}$ gallon for cereal. How much left?

☐ A. $\frac{9}{12}$ gallon
☐ B. $\frac{2}{12}$ gallon
☐ C. $\frac{4}{7}$ gallon
☐ D. $\frac{5}{12}$ gallon

9) Which expression is greater: $(20 - 5) \times 3$ or $20 - (5 \times 3)$?

☐ A. $(20 - 5) \times 3$
☐ B. $20 - (5 \times 3)$
☐ C. The expressions are equal.
☐ D. Cannot be determined.

10) Evaluate: $36 \div (4 + 5) + 6$

☐ A. 4
☐ B. 8
☐ C. 10
☐ D. 15

11) A Venn diagram has circles for "4 equal sides" and "4 right angles." There are 4 rhombuses that are not squares, 5 rectangles that are not squares, and 3 squares. How many figures have 4 equal sides?

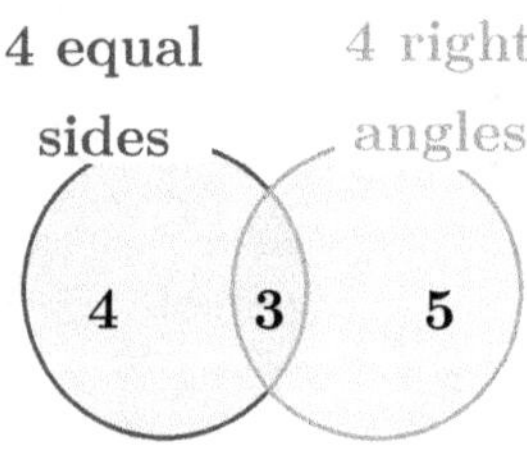

☐ A. 7
☐ B. 8
☐ C. 12
☐ D. 3

12) A prism has $L = 15$ ft, $W = 4$ ft, $H = 6$ ft. Find its volume.

Record your answer in the space provided.

13) Which statement about missing parentheses in $6 + 2 \times 3 - 1$ is true?

Statement
1. The expression equals 16 without parentheses
2. Adding parentheses around $(6 + 2)$ changes the answer
3. Parentheses around 2×3 do not change the answer

☐ A. All statements are true
☐ B. Statements 2 and 3 are true; 1 is false
☐ C. Statements 1 and 2 are true; 3 is false
☐ D. All statements are false

14) Count the unit cubes layer by layer. The first layer has 6 cubes, the second layer has 6 cubes. How many unit cubes are there in total?

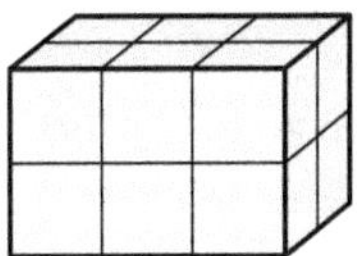

☐ A. 6 unit cubes
☐ B. 12 unit cubes
☐ C. 10 unit cubes
☐ D. 15 unit cubes

15) The line plot shows the amount of juice in several small cups, in ounces:

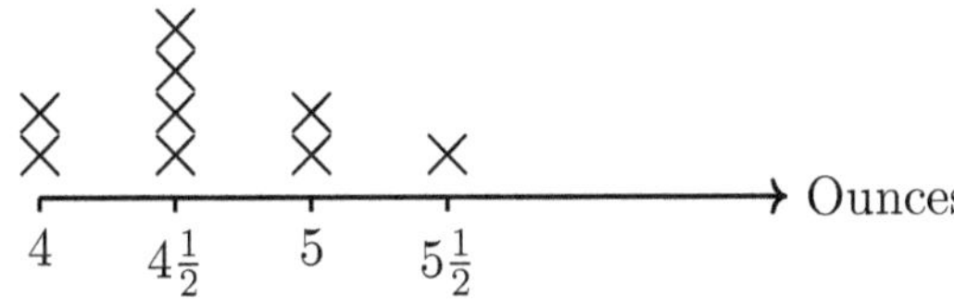

If all the juice is divided into $\frac{1}{2}$-ounce servings, how many servings can be made?

☐ A. 82 servings
☐ B. 83 servings
☐ C. 84 servings
☐ D. 85 servings

16) A rectangular prism has volume 392 cm^3, length 14 cm, and width 7 cm. What is the height?

☐ A. 4 cm
☐ B. 3 cm
☐ C. 2 cm
☐ D. 5 cm

17) Evaluate the expression: $\{36 \div (3+3)\} + \{(2 \times 3) \times 4\}$

Record your answer in the space provided.

18) A box has $V = 210$ ft^3, $l = 7$ ft, $w = 5$ ft. Find its height.

Record your answer in the space provided.

19) A notebook costs \$3.25 and a pen costs \$1.15. Which statements are true? *Select all that apply.*

☐ A. Two notebooks cost \$6.50.
☐ B. One notebook and two pens cost \$5.55.
☐ C. Two notebooks cost \$5.25.
☐ D. Three pens cost \$3.35.

20) Is $4\frac{2}{3} + 5\frac{1}{4}$ closer to 9 or 10?

☐ A. Closer to 8
☐ B. Closer to 9
☐ C. Closer to 10
☐ D. Closer to 11

21) What is 10^2?

☐ A. 10
☐ B. 20
☐ C. 100
☐ D. 1000

22) What is $3.87 + 4.92$?

☐ A. 7.79
☐ B. 8.79
☐ C. 8.69
☐ D. 9.79

23) Without calculating both products, which expression has the larger value?
A: $\frac{2}{3} \times 24$ B: $\frac{4}{5} \times 24$

Record A or B in the space provided.

24) A gardener buys soil in bags. Each bag weighs 25 pounds. She buys 12 bags for one project and 8 bags for another. What is the total weight in tons? Use 1 ton = 2,000 pounds.

☐ A. 4 tons
☐ B. $\frac{1}{2}$ ton
☐ C. 2 tons
☐ D. $\frac{1}{4}$ ton

25) Add three fractions: $\frac{1}{2} + \frac{1}{3} + \frac{1}{6}$

☐ A. $\frac{3}{11}$
☐ B. 1 whole
☐ C. $\frac{5}{6}$
☐ D. $\frac{3}{6}$

26) A recipe uses $\frac{1}{3}$ cup of sugar for one pan. How much sugar is needed for 3 pans?

☐ A. 1 cup
☐ B. $\frac{1}{3}$ cup
☐ C. $\frac{3}{9}$ cup
☐ D. $3\frac{1}{3}$ cups

27) Compute $11.25 - 5.43$.

☐ A. 5.82
☐ B. 6.15
☐ C. 5.72
☐ D. 6.82

28) How many ounces are in 45 pounds?

☐ A. 360 ounces
☐ B. 540 ounces
☐ C. 720 ounces
☐ D. 900 ounces

29) A bakery divides 2,145 cupcakes among 65 catering orders equally. How many cupcakes per order?

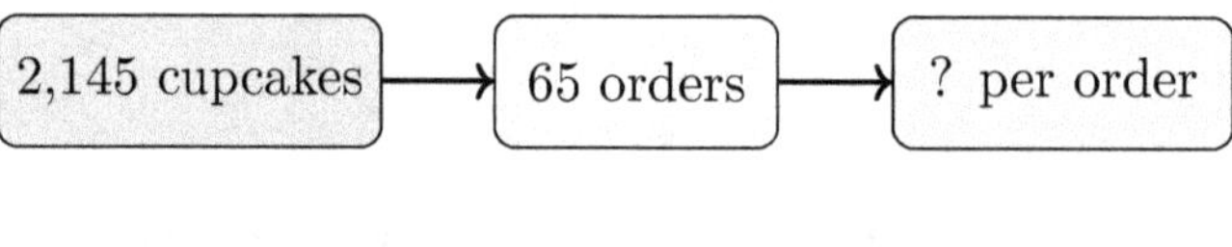

☐ A. 30
☐ B. 32
☐ C. 33
☐ D. 35

30) A measured distance is 24 centimeters. What is this distance in millimeters?

☐ A. 2.4 mm
☐ B. 24 mm
☐ C. 240 mm
☐ D. 2,400 mm

31) Three rectangular prisms each have volume 32 cubic units. Prism A is $2 \times 4 \times 4$. Prism B is $2 \times 2 \times 8$. What are possible dimensions for Prism C?

☐ A. $1 \times 8 \times 4$
☐ B. $1 \times 4 \times 7$
☐ C. $3 \times 4 \times 3$
☐ D. $2 \times 3 \times 5$

32) Which statement describes the location of the point $(2, 6)$ correctly?

☐ A. 2 units left, 6 units down
☐ B. 6 units left, 2 units down
☐ C. 2 units right, 6 units up
☐ D. 6 units right, 2 units up

33) Find: $\frac{1}{4} \div 2$.

Record your answer in the space provided.

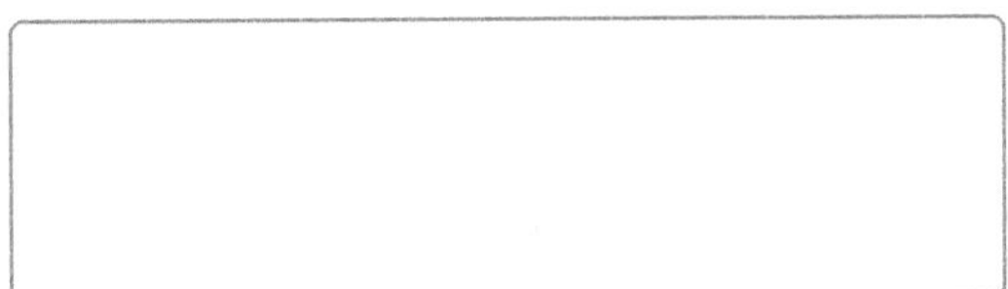

34) A recipe calls for $\frac{1}{4}$-teaspoon portions of salt. How many portions are in 6 teaspoons?

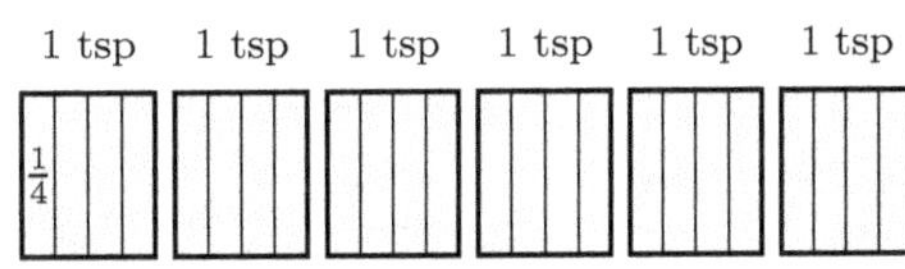

6 teaspoons split into quarter-teaspoon portions

☐ A. 6
☐ B. 12
☐ C. 24
☐ D. 30

35) $0.04 \times 1{,}000 = ?$

☐ A. 0.4
☐ B. 4
☐ C. 40
☐ D. 400

36) The model shows 5 wholes, with each whole cut into pieces of size $\frac{1}{3}$. How many pieces of size $\frac{1}{3}$ are there in all?

1 whole			
1 whole			
1 whole			
1 whole			
1 whole			

5 wholes, each cut into pieces of size $\frac{1}{3}$

☐ A. 15
☐ B. 8
☐ C. 3
☐ D. 5

37) Which statement correctly compares 2.5 and 2.50?

☐ A. $2.5 > 2.50$
☐ B. $2.5 < 2.50$
☐ C. $2.5 \neq 2.50$
☐ D. $2.5 = 2.50$

38) A student lists pairs from the rule "multiply the input by 4, then subtract 2." Which pair does NOT belong?

☐ A. $(1, 2)$
☐ B. $(2, 6)$
☐ C. $(3, 10)$
☐ D. $(4, 15)$

39) Which decimal rounds to 8.3 when rounding to the nearest tenth?

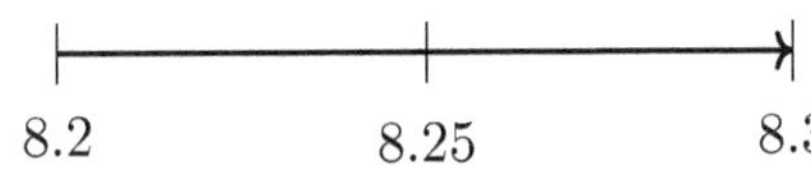

- ☐ A. 8.24
- ☐ B. 8.29
- ☐ C. 8.35
- ☐ D. 8.36

40) A model train tunnel measures 5 meters long, 5 meters wide, and 3 meters tall. What is its volume?

- ☐ A. 25 cubic meters
- ☐ B. 15 cubic meters
- ☐ C. 13 cubic meters
- ☐ D. 75 cubic meters

End of Practice Test

Take a short breath, then check your work with care. Good corrections can teach almost as much as the test itself.

Careful Counter! ✓

You finished a full test. That takes focus and stamina.
Counting twice is faster than fixing one wrong answer.

Count Twice, Move Once ★

Priya had a goal: zero counting mistakes. She used a finger when she counted shapes, dots, or items in a list. Then she counted again to be sure.
It felt slow at first, but her scores jumped. "Two seconds to count again" turned into "two more questions correct."
On 5th grade tests, careful counting matters for problems with charts, graphs, money, and equal groups.

Math Mindset Tip: **Count twice. Move once. That's the safest speed.**

Slow counting is the fastest path to correct counting.
— Math Mindset

Priya's Amazing Journey ★

Priya didn't trust her first count. Not because she wasn't smart, but because counting is easy to slip on.

Imagine counting 17 items in a chart and accidentally skipping one. You'd have 16. Then your answer is one off. A second careful count catches it.

Try the "count twice" habit on your next test. It's free, it's easy, and it pays off.

Priya's Secret: **Trust your second count more than your first.**

Try this on your next practice test. Small, smart habits become big score boosters.

★ Count twice. Smile once. ★

Careful counters become confident solvers.

Grade 5 Math

Grade 5 Mathematics

8

Questions: 40 **Duration:** No time limit

Calculator Policy: Calculators are not allowed

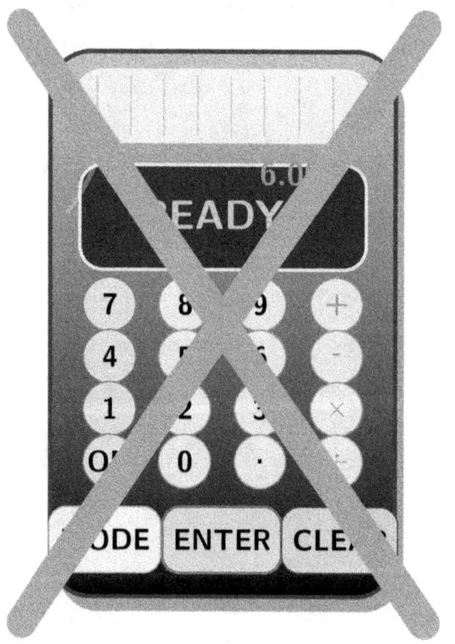

Grade 5 Mathematics Reference Materials

PERIMETER AND AREA

Perimeter of Rectangle	$P = 2l + 2w$ or $P = 2(l + w)$
Area of Rectangle	$A = l \times w$
Area of Triangle	$A = \frac{1}{2} \times b \times h$
Volume of Rectangular Prism	$V = l \times w \times h$

LENGTH

Customary	**Metric**
1 foot (ft) = 12 inches (in.)	1 meter (m) = 100 centimeters (cm)
1 yard (yd) = 3 feet (ft)	1 centimeter (cm) = 10 millimeters (mm)
1 yard (yd) = 36 inches (in.)	1 kilometer (km) = 1,000 meters (m)

CAPACITY

Customary	**Metric**
1 cup (c) = 8 fluid ounces (fl oz)	1 liter (L) = 1,000 milliliters (mL)
1 pint (pt) = 2 cups (c)	
1 quart (qt) = 2 pints (pt)	
1 gallon (gal) = 4 quarts (qt)	

WEIGHT AND MASS

Customary	**Metric**
1 pound (lb) = 16 ounces (oz)	1 kilogram (kg) = 1,000 grams (g)
	1 gram (g) = 1,000 milligrams (mg)

TIME

1 minute (min) = 60 seconds (sec)	1 week = 7 days
1 hour (hr) = 60 minutes (min)	1 year = 12 months
1 day = 24 hours (hr)	1 year = 52 weeks

1) Subtract: $10 - 3\frac{2}{7}$.

☐ A. $6\frac{5}{7}$
☐ B. $6\frac{4}{7}$
☐ C. $7\frac{1}{7}$
☐ D. $7\frac{5}{7}$

2) What is the x-coordinate of $(5, 2)$?

Record your answer in the space provided.

3) A water tank holds 250 liters. It currently has 165.5 liters. How many more liters are needed to fill the tank completely?

☐ A. 74.5 liters
☐ B. 94.5 liters
☐ C. 84.5 liters
☐ D. 104.5 liters

4) Pattern: $15 \times 10 = 150$; $15 \times 100 = 1{,}500$; $15 \times 1{,}000 = ?$

☐ A. 150
☐ B. 1,500
☐ C. 15,000
☐ D. 150,000

5) A warehouse has 27 packs of 100 boxes each. How many boxes total?

☐ A. 127
☐ B. 270
☐ C. 27000
☐ D. 2700

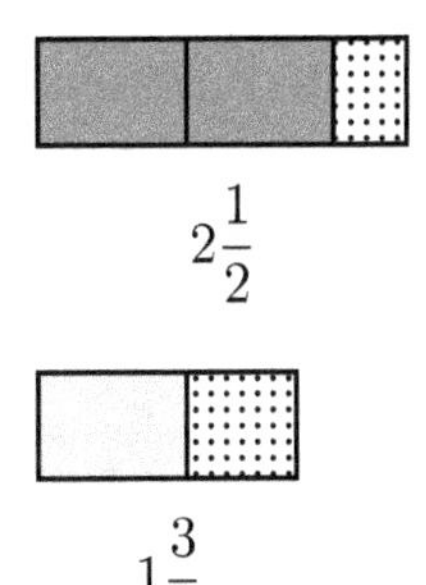

6)

Ribbon lengths: $2\frac{1}{2}$ m and $1\frac{3}{4}$ m. Combined?

☐ A. $3\frac{1}{4}$ m
☐ B. $3\frac{2}{3}$ m
☐ C. $4\frac{1}{4}$ m
☐ D. $4\frac{1}{2}$ m

7) List the first four multiples of 7.

☐ A. 1, 7, 14, 21
☐ B. 7, 14, 21, 35
☐ C. 7, 15, 21, 28
☐ D. 7, 14, 21, 28

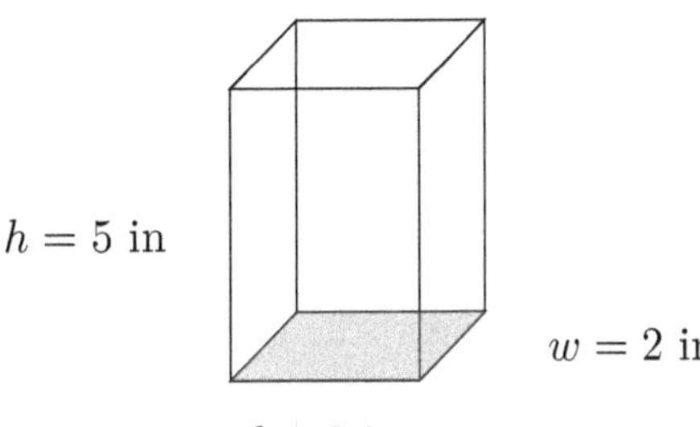

8)

What is the volume?

☐ A. 15 in^3
☐ B. 20 in^3
☐ C. 30 in^3
☐ D. 10 in^3

9) For the points $(1, 2), (2, 4), (3, 6)$, each Y value is how many times X?

Record your answer in the space provided.

10) Which expression is $\frac{1}{5}$ of $(100 - 25)$?

☐ A. $(100 - 25) \times 5$
☐ B. $(100 - 25) \div 5$
☐ C. $100 - (25 \div 5)$
☐ D. $5 \div (100 - 25)$

11) Find: $1 \times \frac{5}{9}$.

Record your answer in the space provided.

12) A gardener plants on $\frac{3}{8}$ of land initially, then $\frac{1}{8}$ more. Fraction planted?

☐ A. $\frac{2}{8}$
☐ B. $\frac{7}{8}$
☐ C. $\frac{5}{8}$
☐ D. $\frac{1}{2}$

13) A student says that in the number 2.894, the digit 4 is worth 0.4. What error did the student make?

☐ A. The student read the digit in the wrong place; 4 is in the thousandths place, so it is worth 0.004.
☐ B. The student forgot to subtract before reading place values.
☐ C. The student correctly identified the value.
☐ D. The student confused tenths and ones.

14) Which expression has a value of 12?

A	B
$4 \times (3+2)$	$(4+2) \times 3$
C	**D**
$2 \times (3+3)$	$3 \times (2+3)$

☐ A. $4 \times (3+2)$

☐ B. $(4+2) \times 3$

☐ C. $2 \times (3+3)$

☐ D. $3 \times (2+3)$

15) Which expression equals 0.042?

☐ A. $42 \div 10$

☐ B. $4.2 \div 10$

☐ C. $42 \div 100$

☐ D. $4.2 \div 100$

16) A rectangular aquarium has a volume of 360 cubic inches. If the base is 10 inches by 9 inches, what is the height of the aquarium?

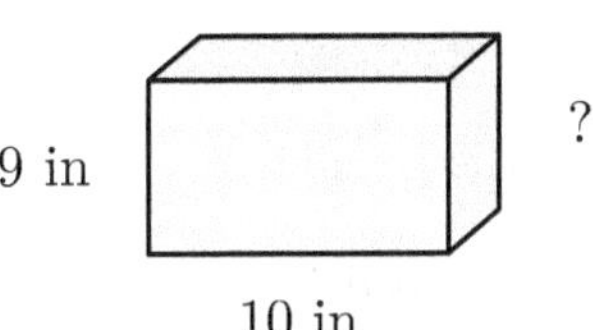

☐ A. 2 inches

☐ B. 8 inches

☐ C. 6 inches

☐ D. 4 inches

17) A race is 16 miles long. A runner completes $\frac{3}{4}$ of the race. Then the runner completes $\frac{1}{2}$ of the distance still remaining. How many miles has the runner covered in all?

☐ A. 12 miles

☐ B. 14 miles

☐ C. 16 miles

☐ D. 18 miles

18) True or false: $0.032 \times 10^2 = 3.2$?

☐ A. True
☐ B. False, it equals 32
☐ C. False, it equals 0.32
☐ D. False, it equals 320

19) A store has $\frac{2}{5}$ of its shelf space dedicated to pasta. Of that space, $\frac{3}{4}$ is stocked with spaghetti. What fraction of the total shelf is spaghetti?

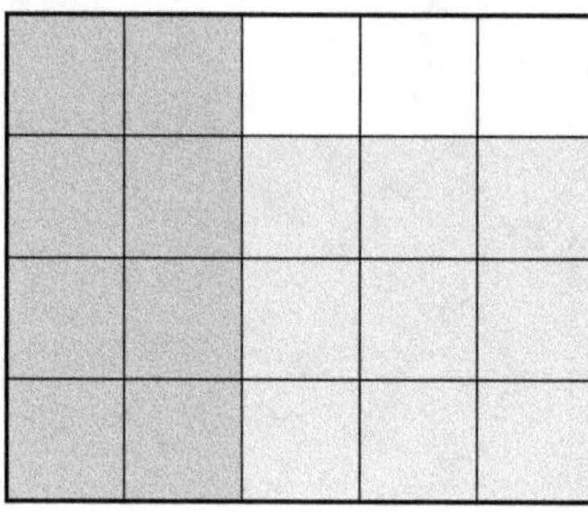

☐ A. $\frac{6}{20}$ or $\frac{3}{10}$
☐ B. $\frac{1}{5}$
☐ C. $\frac{5}{9}$
☐ D. $\frac{2}{3}$

20) The line plot shows ribbon lengths in inches:

Ribbon Lengths

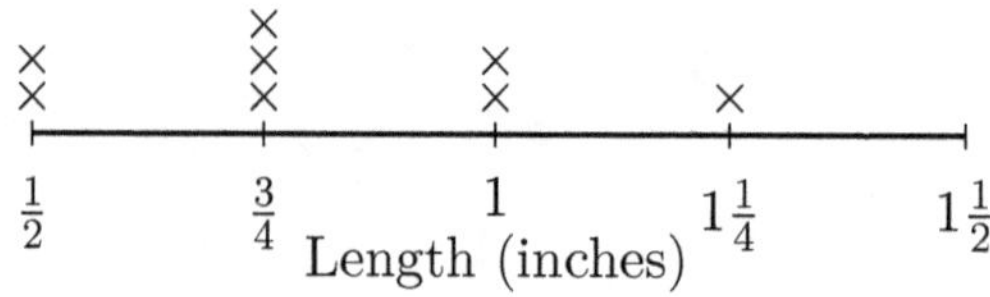

What is the total length of the two ribbons that each measure $\frac{1}{2}$ inch?

☐ A. 1 inch
☐ B. $\frac{1}{2}$ inch
☐ C. $\frac{3}{4}$ inch
☐ D. 2 inches

21) What is $\frac{1}{2}$ of $\frac{3}{4}$ of a class (in simplest form)?

☐ A. $\frac{3}{8}$
☐ B. $\frac{3}{6}$
☐ C. $\frac{4}{6}$
☐ D. $\frac{1}{6}$

22) Select all that apply. Which statements describe good volume work for a composite solid?

☐ A. Add volumes of non-overlapping prism parts.
☐ B. Label the answer in cubic units.
☐ C. Multiply length, width, and height for each part.
☐ D. Label the answer in square units.

23) An area model shows 3.2×2.5. Break it into whole and decimal parts and find the total.

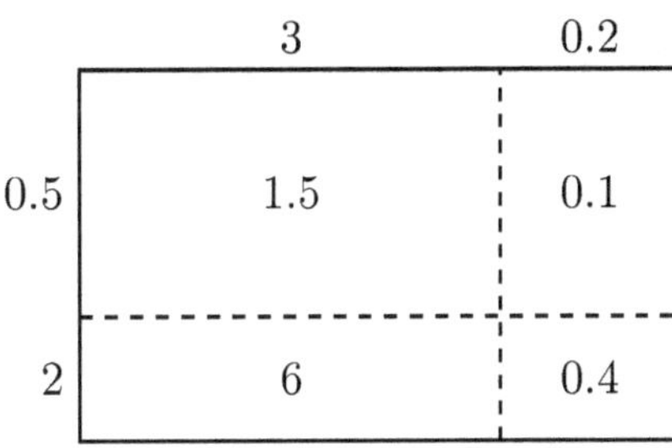

☐ A. 7.5
☐ B. 8
☐ C. 8.5
☐ D. 9

24) A ribbon is $\frac{1}{5}$ meter long. It is cut into 4 equal pieces. How long is each piece?

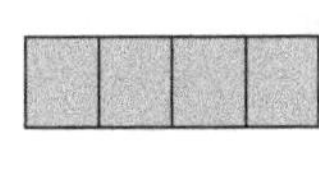

$\frac{1}{5}$ m

☐ A. $\frac{1}{20}$ meter
☐ B. $\frac{4}{5}$ meter
☐ C. $\frac{1}{1}$ meter
☐ D. $\frac{1}{9}$ meter

25) Pattern A: $0, 5, 10, 15, 20$. Pattern B: $0, 1, 2, 3, 4$. For the nonzero matching terms, each A value is how many times the corresponding B value?

Record your answer in the space provided.

26) A polygon has 6 sides, 6 vertices, and all sides and angles equal. What name can be used for this shape?

Record your answer in the space provided.

27) Which factor will make $28 \times$ factor less than 28?

$\frac{6}{5} > 1$ | $\frac{9}{9} = 1$ | $\frac{5}{7} < 1$ | $1\frac{1}{5} > 1$

Compare each factor to 1

- ☐ A. $\frac{6}{5}$
- ☐ B. $\frac{9}{9}$
- ☐ C. $\frac{5}{7}$
- ☐ D. $1\frac{1}{5}$

28) A piece of string is 7 meters long. How many $\frac{1}{4}$-meter pieces can be cut?

7 meters

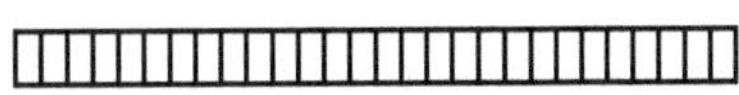

$\frac{1}{4}$ m

☐ A. 16 pieces
☐ B. 20 pieces
☐ C. 24 pieces
☐ D. 28 pieces

29) Maria has 8 pizzas. Each person gets one fourth of a pizza. Which division equation matches the situation?

☐ A. $\frac{1}{4} \div 8 = n$
☐ B. $8 \times \frac{1}{4} = n$
☐ C. $8 + \frac{1}{4} = n$
☐ D. $8 \div \frac{1}{4} = n$

30) In the number 6.482, what is the place value of the digit 8?

6.482

☐ A. Tenths
☐ B. Hundredths
☐ C. Thousandths
☐ D. Ones

31) A graph shows hours studied on the x-axis and test scores on the y-axis. Point $(5, 85)$ is plotted on the graph. What does this point represent?

☐ A. A student studied for 85 hours and scored 5 points
☐ B. A test took 5 hours and had 85 questions
☐ C. A student scored 5 points and studied for 85 hours
☐ D. A student studied for 5 hours and scored 85 points

32) A rectangular prism has a base area of 48 ft^2 and height 5 ft. What is the volume?

☐ A. 200 ft^3
☐ B. 220 ft^3
☐ C. 240 ft^3
☐ D. 260 ft^3

33) The table shows a pattern. What is the missing value?

Input	Output
1	7
2	14
3	21
4	?

☐ A. 24
☐ B. 28
☐ C. 30
☐ D. 32

34) Which fraction is equivalent to $\frac{2}{10}$ in simplest form?

☐ A. $\frac{1}{5}$
☐ B. $\frac{2}{5}$
☐ C. $\frac{1}{10}$
☐ D. $\frac{2}{20}$

35) A recipe calls for $\frac{1}{3}$ cup of oil. How much oil is needed to make $3\frac{1}{3}$ times the recipe?

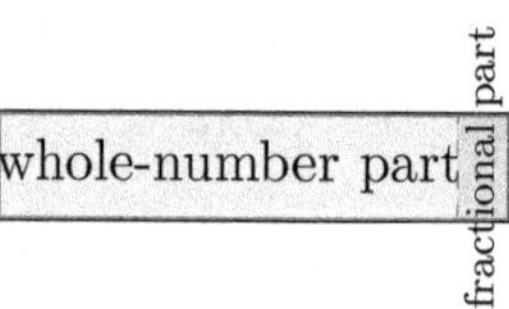

☐ A. $1\frac{1}{9}$ cups
☐ B. $1\frac{1}{3}$ cups
☐ C. 1 cup
☐ D. $\frac{2}{3}$ cup

36) A right triangle has angles of 90 degrees, 60 degrees, and 30 degrees. Can it be isosceles?

☐ A. Yes, all right triangles are isosceles
☐ B. Cannot be determined
☐ C. Yes, because it is a right triangle
☐ D. No, because it has no equal angles

37) What is 23×11?

☐ A. 245
☐ B. 253
☐ C. 261
☐ D. 269

38) Subtract and simplify: $\frac{11}{12} - \frac{1}{4}$

☐ A. $\frac{10}{12}$
☐ B. $\frac{7}{12}$
☐ C. $\frac{2}{3}$
☐ D. $\frac{5}{12}$

39) True or False: Every parallelogram is a quadrilateral.

☐ A. True, because parallelograms have four sides.
☐ B. False, because parallelograms have more than four sides.
☐ C. True, only for squares.
☐ D. False, because they are not polygons.

40) Which expression is greater: $4 \times (15 + 7)$ or $4 \times 15 + 7$?

☐ A. $4 \times (15 + 7)$
☐ B. $4 \times 15 + 7$
☐ C. The expressions are equal.
☐ D. Cannot be determined.

End of Practice Test

Take a short breath, then check your work with care. Good corrections can teach almost as much as the test itself.

Time Traveler Triumph!

You've Journeyed Through All 8 Practice Tests!

You're a Math Time Traveler!

Time-jump complete! You traveled through all 8 practice tests—that's 320 math problems. With each leap, you added new skills to your math toolkit and grew braver under pressure.

Your Time-Traveling Triumphs:

- Time-traveled through 8 full practice tests (320 questions!)
- Built stamina for a full 40-question test
- Practiced strategy and steady checking
- Learned from past mistakes and re-wrote them as wins
- Built confidence that lasts through any era

Your timeline looks bright! On test day, you'll bring everything you've practiced.

Your Time-Travel Log!

Mark Each Stop on Your Timeline

Record the date and score for each leap:

Test	Date	Score	Notes
Test 1		/40	
Test 2		/40	
Test 3		/40	
Test 4		/40	
Test 5		/40	
Test 6		/40	
Test 7		/40	
Test 8		/40	

Time Traveler's Thoughts:

- Which test felt like the wildest leap?
- Which strategy from the past helped you the most?
- What would you tell yourself before Test 1?
- How will you use these skills in the future?

Test-day tip: Read carefully, show your work, and check that your answer makes sense.

Your math journey across time is just beginning. Keep leaping!

Practice Test Answer Keys

How to use this section:

1. check your answer
2. circle missed questions
3. rework them before reading the explanation

Good correction habits build strong scores.

Answer Key for Practice Test 1

Question	Answer
1	C
2	D
3	A
4	C
5	C
6	C
7	B
8	0.04
9	D
10	C
11	B
12	3
13	B
14	C
15	B
16	B
17	D
18	A, B
19	C
20	C
21	D
22	D
23	C
24	A
25	A
26	60
27	D
28	25000
29	A
30	C
31	D
32	A
33	A
34	0.55
35	B
36	D
37	C
38	D
39	D
40	A

Answer Key for Practice Test 2

Question	Answer
1	B
2	B
3	A
4	D
5	B
6	D
7	D
8	A
9	B
10	D
11	C
12	C
13	$395.50
14	A
15	B
16	A
17	$\frac{1}{4}$
18	B
19	12
20	C
21	A, B
22	A
23	D
24	B
25	A
26	C
27	B
28	D
29	A
30	D
31	C
32	$2\frac{1}{2}$ m
33	20
34	B
35	A
36	D
37	B
38	C
39	B
40	B

Answer Key for Practice Test 3

#	Answer	#	Answer
1	D	26	C
2	C	27	D
3	B	28	C
4	D	29	D
5	B	30	A
6	C	31	A
7	D	32	D
8	A	33	80
9	A	34	C
10	4	35	B
11	C	36	C
12	C	37	D
13	2	38	D
14	720000	39	A
15	A	40	D
16	D		
17	D		
18	A, C		
19	A		
20	C		
21	D		
22	B		
23	D		
24	D		
25	56		

Answer Key for Practice Test 4

#	Answer	#	Answer
1	C	26	about 1
2	C	27	A
3	D	28	7
4	A	29	C
5	B	30	D
6	D	31	$33\frac{3}{4}$ in
7	B	32	B
8	C	33	A
9	C	34	A
10	D	35	A
11	D	36	D
12	A	37	B
13	8.2	38	B
14	A	39	C
15	B	40	D
16	A		
17	D		
18	B		
19	D		
20	C		
21	$(6 \times 10) \div 2$		
22	A, B		
23	C		
24	C		
25	B		

Answer Key for Practice Test 5

#	Answer	#	Answer
1	C	26	D
2	C	27	18
3	A	28	D
4	D	29	B
5	0.07	30	2400
6	B	31	D
7	C	32	A
8	20	33	C
9	B	34	B
10	B	35	B
11	C	36	C
12	C	37	D
13	C	38	C
14	B	39	D
15	A	40	D
16	D		
17	12.009		
18	B		
19	C		
20	D		
21	A, B		
22	D		
23	B		
24	D		
25	B		

Answer Key for Practice Test 6

#	Answer	#	Answer
1	B	26	C
2	D	27	D
3	D	28	A
4	C	29	C
5	D	30	C
6	C	31	C
7	42	32	C
8	21	33	0.24
9	D	34	B
10	B	35	D
11	A	36	A
12	5	37	C
13	B	38	700
14	B	39	A
15	C	40	B
16	C		
17	B		
18	A, B		
19	C		
20	C		
21	A		
22	B		
23	D		
24	A		
25	D		

Answer Key for Practice Test 7

Question	Answer	Question	Answer
1	A	26	A
2	C	27	A
3	B	28	C
4	D	29	C
5	C	30	C
6	C	31	A
7	D	32	C
8	D	33	$\frac{1}{8}$
9	A	34	C
10	C	35	C
11	A	36	A
12	360 ft^3	37	D
13	B	38	D
14	B	39	B
15	B	40	D
16	A		
17	30		
18	6 ft		
19	A, B		
20	C		
21	C		
22	B		
23	B		
24	D		
25	B		

Answer Key for Practice Test 8

Question	Answer	Question	Answer
1	A	26	hexagon
2	5	27	C
3	C	28	D
4	C	29	D
5	D	30	B
6	C	31	D
7	D	32	C
8	C	33	B
9	2	34	A
10	B	35	A
11	$\frac{5}{9}$	36	D
12	D	37	B
13	A	38	C
14	C	39	A
15	D	40	A
16	D		
17	B		
18	A		
19	A		
20	A		
21	A		
22	A, B, C		
23	B		
24	A		
25	5		

Practice Test Answers and Explanations

Practice Test 1 Answers and Explanations

1) **Choice C is correct.** 5.NF.7b $3 \div \frac{1}{3} = 3 \times 3 = 9$. There are 9 segments.
2) **Choice D is correct.** 5.NBT.2 $5 \times 10^4 = 50000$ has 5 in the ten-thousands place.
3) **Choice A is correct.** 5.MD.5a One prism: $4 \times 5 \times 3 = 60$ in^3. Three prisms: $60 \times 3 = 180$ in^3.
4) **Choice C is correct.** 5.NF.7c The unit fraction is the amount being shared, so divide $\frac{1}{6}$ by 5. The equation is $\frac{1}{6} \div 5 = n$.
5) **Choice C is correct.** 5.MD.2 The labels are in half-inches. The total is $(2\times4)+(4\times2)+(6\times2)+(8\times1)+(10\times1) = 46$ half-inches. Since 2 half-inches make 1 inch, $46 \div 2 = 23$ inches.
6) **Choice C is correct.** 5.NF.7c The strip starts with one eighth, then shares that small amount into 3 parts. So the matching division equation is $\frac{1}{8} \div 3 = ?$.
7) **Choice B is correct.** 5.NF.1 Add: $3\frac{2}{5} + 2\frac{3}{5} = 5\frac{5}{5} = 6$ yd.
8) **The correct answer is 0.04.** 5.NBT.2 Move the decimal point one place left: $0.4 \rightarrow 0.04$.
9) **Choice D is correct.** 5.NBT.2 Prism A: $3\times4\times5 = 60$ cu. in. Prism B: $3\times4\times3 = 36$ cu. in. Difference: $60-36 = 24$ cu. in.
10) **Choice C is correct.** 5.NF.2 The list for 10 reaches 90, and the list for 9 also reaches 90. No smaller number appears in both lists, so the LCD is 90.
11) **Choice B is correct.** 5.MD.5 The base layer has $8 \times 4 = 32$ square units. Divide the volume by the base area: $128 \div 32 = 4$, so the height is 4 inches.
12) **The correct answer is 3.** 5.G.2 For nonzero terms, $9 \div 3 = 3$, $18 \div 6 = 3$, and $27 \div 9 = 3$.
13) **Choice B is correct.** 5.G.2 $\frac{1}{6} \div 2 = \frac{1}{12}$ m.
14) **Choice C is correct.** 5.NF.5b Since $\frac{5}{3} > 1$, multiplying by it makes the result greater than 12.
15) **Choice B is correct.** 5.G.4 A rhombus is a quadrilateral with all sides equal. If opposite angles are also equal, it is a rhombus (not necessarily a square).
16) **Choice B is correct.** 5.G.2 Point X is 9 units right and 1 unit up, matching the coordinates $(9, 1)$.
17) **Choice D is correct.** 5.NF.2 Multiply both the numerator and the denominator of $\frac{3}{5}$ by 2: $\frac{3\times2}{5\times2} = \frac{6}{10}$. So $\frac{3}{5}$ and $\frac{6}{10}$ are equivalent.
18) **Choices A, B are correct.** 5.NBT.4 3.17 and 3.24 both round to 3.2 to the nearest tenth. 3.25 rounds up to 3.3, and 3.09 rounds to 3.1.
19) **Choice C is correct.** 5.MD.5a Compute each volume: $P = 5\times4\times6 = 120$; $Q = 10\times3\times5 = 150$; $R = 8\times6\times2 = 96$; $S = 4\times4\times6 = 96$. Only R and S have the same volume (96 cubic units).
20) **Choice C is correct.** 5.NF.2 Use a common denominator of 24: $\frac{5}{6} = \frac{20}{24}$ and $\frac{3}{8} = \frac{9}{24}$. Then $\frac{20}{24} - \frac{9}{24} = \frac{11}{24}$ yard.
21) **Choice D is correct.** 5.G.2 First ordered pair: (Pattern 1 first value, Pattern 2 first value) = (5, 2).
22) **Choice D is correct.** 5.NBT.2 The blank must make the product end with exactly 2 zeros. $3 \times 200 = 600$, and 600 has exactly 2 zeros.
23) **Choice C is correct.** 5.NBT.7 Multiply: $56 \times 15 = 840$, then place decimal two places from right: $8.40 = 8.4$.
24) **Choice A is correct.** 5.NBT.7 Round: $823 \approx 800$ and $41 \approx 40$. So $800 \div 40 = 20$. Actual: $823 \div 41 = 20$ R3.
25) **Choice A is correct.** 5.G.4 An equilateral triangle is classified by its side lengths: all three sides are equal.
26) **The correct answer is 60.** 5.MD.4 Multiply the number of cubes in each layer by the number of layers: $12 \times 5 = 60$. The volume is 60 cubic units.
27) **Choice D is correct.** 5.MD.4 Since 1 pound = 16 ounces, multiply 4 by 16: $4 \times 16 = 64$ ounces.
28) **The correct answer is 25000.** 5.NBT.2 Multiplying by a power of 10 shifts the value to a larger place. $250 \times 100 =$ 25,000 (attach two zeros). This confirms the answer.
29) **Choice A is correct.** 5.NBT.2 Count the X marks above each height. The height $2\frac{1}{4}$ cm has only 1 mark, so it is the least common.

30) **Choice C is correct.** 5.G.2 Both stores have the same y-coordinate (5), so the distance is measured horizontally. The distance is $7 - 2 = 5$ blocks.

31) **Choice D is correct.** 5.MD.1 Two servings is $\frac{1}{4}$ of 8 servings. The full recipe uses 20 fluid ounces, so $20 \div 4 = 5$ fluid ounces.

32) **Choice A is correct.** 5.MD.5a The base area is $10 \times 4 = 40$ square meters. Since $280 \div 40 = 7$, the height is 7 m.

33) **Choice A is correct.** 5.NBT.3a $2 \times 1 = 2$; $3 \times \frac{1}{10} = 0.3$; $7 \times \frac{1}{100} = 0.07$. So $2 + 0.3 + 0.07 = 2.37$.

34) **The correct answer is 0.55.** 5.NBT.3b Compare as thousandths: 0.600, 0.550, and 0.605. The least is 0.55.

35) **Choice B is correct.** 5.NBT.3b Do the division and multiplication first: $72 \div 8 = 9$ and $3 \times 3 = 9$. Then finish left to right: $9 + 9 - 5 = 13$.

36) **Choice D is correct.** 5.NF.5b $50 \times \frac{3}{10} = 15$ liters. Multiplying by $\frac{3}{10}$ (less than 1) gives a smaller result.

37) **Choice C is correct.** 5.NBT.1 In 15.375, the decimal digits are: 3 (tenths), 7 (hundredths), 5 (thousandths). The digit in the hundredths place is 7.

38) **Choice D is correct.** 5.MD.5c Each rectangular prism needs length times width times height. Since the prisms do not overlap, the two volumes are added.

39) **Choice D is correct.** 5.NBT.2 Multiplying by 10 moves the decimal 1 place right: $0.36 \times 10 = 3.6$.

40) **Choice A is correct.** 5.OA.1 To make 20, group the addition first: $(6 + 4) \times 2 = 10 \times 2 = 20$. The other choices give different values, so A is the only match.

Practice Test 2 Answers and Explanations

1) **Choice B is correct.** 5.NBT.6 $936 \div 13 = 72$ packs. Check: $13 \times 72 = 936$.

2) **Choice B is correct.** 5.NF.1 LCM(7,4) = 28. $\frac{2}{7} = \frac{8}{28}$ and $\frac{3}{4} = \frac{21}{28}$. $\frac{8}{28} + \frac{21}{28} = \frac{29}{28} = 1\frac{1}{28}$.

3) **Choice A is correct.** 5.MD.5 The base area is $8 \times 6 = 48$ square centimeters. Since $240 \div 48 = 5$, the height is 5 cm.

4) **Choice D is correct.** 5.OA.3 The numbers do not increase by the same amount each time; instead, each term is doubled. Since $10 \times 2 = 20$, $20 \times 2 = 40$, and $40 \times 2 = 80$, the rule is multiply by 2.

5) **Choice B is correct.** 5.NBT.2 Compute each pair. A: $3{,}000 \div 10 = 300$ and $300 \div 10 = 30$ ($300 \neq 30$). B: $2{,}100 \div 100 = 21$ and $210 \div 10 = 21$ — both equal 21 ✓. C: $5{,}600 \div 1{,}000 = 5.6$ and $56 \div 100 = 0.56$ ($5.6 \neq 0.56$). D: $1{,}500 \div 100 = 15$ and $1{,}500 \div 1{,}000 = 1.5$ ($15 \neq 1.5$).

6) **Choice D is correct.** 5.NF.5b $2\frac{1}{2} \times 12 = \frac{5}{2} \times 12 = \frac{60}{2} = 30$ inches.

7) **Choice D is correct.** 5.MD.5 Total people: $28 + 4 = 32$. Empty seats: $40 - 32 = 8$ seats.

8) **Choice A is correct.** 5.OA.3 Pattern R is 5 times Pattern S: $2 \times 5 = 10$, $4 \times 5 = 20$, $6 \times 5 = 30$, $8 \times 5 = 40$.

9) **Choice B is correct.** 5.NBT.5 Multiply: $214 \times 2 = (200 \times 2) + (10 \times 2) + (4 \times 2) = 400 + 20 + 8 = 428$.

10) **Choice D is correct.** 5.NBT.5 Points on the same horizontal grid line have the same second coordinate, but their first coordinates can be different. Points A, B, C are all 5 units above the x-axis and have first coordinates 2, 5, and 8.

11) **Choice C is correct.** 5.OA.2 The first expression has 7 groups of 25 plus 7 groups of 5. That is the same as 7 groups of the combined amount $(25 + 5)$.

12) **Choice C is correct.** 5.NBT.2 $15 \times 10^3 = 15 \times 1000 = 15000$ meters.

13) **The correct answer is $395.50.** 5.NBT.7 Line up the decimal points and add the two money amounts: $189.00 + $206.50 = $395.50. So the sandwich shop earned $395.50 in all.

14) **Choice A is correct.** 5.OA.2 Dividing by 2 makes the second half as large, so the first is twice the second.

15) **Choice B is correct.** 5.MD.1 1 m = 100 cm. Multiply: $1.35 \times 100 = 135$ cm.

16) **Choice A is correct.** 5.NF.7c The unit fraction is the amount being shared, so divide $\frac{1}{10}$ by 2. The equation is $\frac{1}{10} \div 2 = n$.

17) **The correct answer is $\frac{1}{4}$.** 5.NF.5b Multiply first: $\frac{5 \times 3}{6 \times 10} = \frac{15}{60}$. Since 15 is one fourth of 60, the product is $\frac{1}{4}$.

18) **Choice B is correct.** 5.NF.5b Dividing by 100 moves the decimal two places left, so 720 becomes 7.2.

19) **The correct answer is 12.** 5.NBT.2 You can multiply first: $\frac{4}{5} \times 15 = \frac{60}{5} = 12$. You can also think of $\frac{1}{5}$ of 15 as 3, so $\frac{4}{5}$ of 15 is 4 groups of 3, or 12.

20) **Choice C is correct.** 5.NF.4 Small: $3 \times 2 \times 8 = 48$ cubic feet. Large: $4 \times 3 \times 8 = 96$ cubic feet. Difference: $96 - 48 = 48$ cubic feet.

21) **Choices A, B are correct.** (5.NF.2) $\frac{3}{4}+\frac{1}{2}=1\frac{1}{4}$, so A is true. Since $1\frac{1}{4}$ is more than 1, B is also true. C multiplies; D ignores the second trip.

22) **Choice A is correct.** (5.NF.1) Convert to eighths: $1\frac{4}{8}+3\frac{3}{8}=4\frac{7}{8}$.

23) **Choice D is correct.** (5.NF.2) Multiples of 4: 4, 8, 12, ... Multiples of 6: 6, 12, 18, ... The LCM is 12.

24) **Choice B is correct.** (5.NF.2) $\frac{11}{12}$ is close to 1, and $\frac{2}{7}$ is closer to $\frac{1}{2}$ than to 0. So $\frac{11}{12}-\frac{2}{7}\approx 1-\frac{1}{2}=\frac{1}{2}$.

25) **Choice A is correct.** (5.MD.5) Use the rectangular-prism volume formula: $10\times 3\times 4=120$. So the volume is 120 cubic centimeters.

26) **Choice C is correct.** (5.G.3) An octagon has 8 sides and 8 vertices. (A pentagon has 5, a hexagon has 6, a nonagon has 9.)

27) **Choice B is correct.** (5.G.3) One prism: $3\times 4\times 2=24$ cm^3. Three prisms: $24\times 3=72$ cm^3.

28) **Choice D is correct.** (5.NF.4b) Paint used $=\frac{5}{8}\times\frac{2}{5}=\frac{10}{40}$ of a full can.

29) **Choice A is correct.** (5.NBT.3b) All have 6 ones. Compare the tenths and hundredths: $6.02<6.18<6.35<6.50$.

30) **Choice D is correct.** (5.NBT.7) Line up decimal points and subtract place by place. $9.50-4.07=5.43$ gallons. This confirms the answer.

31) **Choice C is correct.** (5.NBT.4) The hundredths digit is 3. The thousandths digit is 5. Since $5\geq 5$, round hundredths up: $3\rightarrow 4$, giving 7.64 g.

32) **The correct answer is $2\frac{1}{2}$ m.** (5.NF.6) $3\times\frac{5}{6}=\frac{15}{6}=\frac{5}{2}=2\frac{1}{2}$ m.

33) **The correct answer is 20.** (5.NF.6) $5\div\frac{1}{4}=20$. Each pound makes 4 quarter-pound loaves, so 5 pounds makes 20 loaves.

34) **Choice B is correct.** (5.NF.7c) Dividing by 10: $52.3\div 10=5.23$ kg per classroom.

35) **Choice A is correct.** (5.MD.2) The bottles contain $2(8)+3(8\frac{1}{2})+3(9)+1(9\frac{1}{2})=16+25\frac{1}{2}+27+9\frac{1}{2}=78$ ounces.

36) **Choice D is correct.** (5.NBT.2) Multiplying by 100 makes the value 100 times as large: $78\times 100=7{,}800$.

37) **Choice B is correct.** (5.NBT.2) $2\times 3\times 6=36$ unit cubes. The other products do not equal 36.

38) **Choice C is correct.** (5.OA.2) Choice C works because $4\times(6+2)$ can be split into $4\times 6+4\times 2$. Both expressions have the same value, 32.

39) **Choice B is correct.** (5.NF.1) Student B did not regroup before subtracting the fractions, so the whole-number part is too large. The correct difference is $2\frac{2}{4}=2\frac{1}{2}$.

40) **Choice B is correct.** (5.G.2) If the inputs start at 1, the 5th pair uses input 5. The output is $5+4=9$, so the pair is $(5,9)$.

Practice Test 3 Answers and Explanations

1) **Choice D is correct.** (5.OA.3) Pattern Kappa is 3 times Pattern Iota: $3\times 3=9$, $6\times 3=18$, $9\times 3=27$, $12\times 3=36$, $15\times 3=45$.

2) **Choice C is correct.** (5.NF.6) $\frac{3}{5}\times 120=\frac{3\times 120}{5}=\frac{360}{5}=72$ pounds.

3) **Choice B is correct.** (5.NBT.7) Add: \$3.29 + \$2.74 = \$6.03 (hundredths: $9+4=13$, regroup; tenths: $2+7+1=10$, regroup; dollars: $3+2+1=6$).

4) **Choice D is correct.** (5.NF.2) Convert to common denominator 6: $\frac{1}{6}=\frac{1}{6}$ and $\frac{2}{3}=\frac{4}{6}$. Since $\frac{4}{6}>\frac{1}{6}$, water is more.

5) **Choice B is correct.** (5.NF.4) There are 5 groups of $\frac{2}{7}$, so multiply 5×2 in the numerator: $5\times\frac{2}{7}=\frac{10}{7}=1\frac{3}{7}$.

6) **Choice C is correct.** (5.NF.7c) Start with one unit fraction, $\frac{1}{4}$, and share it into 4 equal parts. Each part is $\frac{1}{4}\div 4=\frac{1}{16}$ of the whole.

7) **Choice D is correct.** (5.NF.7c) The size of each group is $\frac{1}{4}$ yard. $6\div\frac{1}{4}=6\times 4=24$ beds.

8) **Choice A is correct.** (5.NF.5b) $\frac{1}{3}\times\frac{3}{4}=\frac{3}{12}=\frac{1}{4}$ pound.

9) **Choice A is correct.** (5.MD.5a) Volume requires multiplication: $V=4\times 3\times 6=72$ m^3, not addition.

10) **The correct answer is 4.** (5.G.4) A square is a quadrilateral, a rectangle, a rhombus, and a parallelogram.

11) **Choice C is correct.** (5.G.4) A parallelogram with all sides equal is a rhombus. This is the most specific classification.

12) **Choice C is correct.** (5.MD.5a) Prism X: $4\times 5\times 6=120$ cm^3. Prism Y: $3\times 5\times 8=120$ cm^3. Both are equal.

13) **The correct answer is 2.** (5.G.1) Point P is inside Quadrant I, so its x-coordinate and y-coordinate are both positive. Points on an axis can have a 0 coordinate, but this point is not on an axis.

14) **The correct answer is 720000.** (5.NBT.2) Use $8 \times 9 = 72$. The factors 80 and 9,000 have four zeros total, so the product is 720,000.
15) **Choice A is correct.** (5.NBT.2) Find the total spent before subtracting from 50. The 3 items cost $3 \times 5 = 15$, lunch costs \$7, and together that is $15 + 7 = 22$. The expression $50 - [(3 \times 5) + 7]$ shows the money left.
16) **Choice D is correct.** (5.NBT.5) Multiply: $304 \times 2 = (300 \times 2) + (4 \times 2) = 600 + 8 = 608$.
17) **Choice D is correct.** (5.G.2) The x-coordinate (7) is the number of weeks, and the y-coordinate (35) is the amount saved in dollars. So \$35 was saved after 7 weeks.
18) **Choices A, C are correct.** (5.OA.1) Start with the grouped addition: $8 + 4 = 12$. Then $12 \div 2 = 6$, and $6 + 1 = 7$, so A and C are true. Choice B skips the grouping, and choice D gives the wrong final value.
19) **Choice A is correct.** (5.NF.7a) $\frac{1}{10} \div 3 = \frac{1}{10} \times \frac{1}{3} = \frac{1}{30}$.
20) **Choice C is correct.** (5.MD.2) Count X marks above $\frac{3}{8}$ on the line plot. There are 4 X marks.
21) **Choice D is correct.** (5.MD.5c) Find each part first: Prism A is $5 \times 4 \times 3 = 60$ cubic meters, and Prism B is $6 \times 2 \times 5 = 60$ cubic meters. Because the parts do not overlap, add them: $60 + 60 = 120$ cubic meters.
22) **Choice B is correct.** (5.NF.5b) $30 \times \frac{2}{3} = 20$ feet. Since $\frac{2}{3} < 1$, the painted length is less than 30 feet.
23) **Choice D is correct.** (5.NBT.2) Option D is false because $0.023 \times 1000 = 23$. The others are correct.
24) **Choice D is correct.** (5.NBT.3a) 0.309 has 3 in tenths and 9 in thousandths. Since there are 0 hundredths, the expanded form can omit the hundredths term: $\frac{3}{10} + \frac{9}{1000} = 0.309$.
25) **The correct answer is 56.** (5.NBT.2) $10^2 = 100$. Dividing by 100 removes two zeros (or moves decimal two places left): $5{,}600 \rightarrow 56$.
26) **Choice C is correct.** (5.NBT.2) Total: $8.5 + 12.3 + 9.7 + 10.5 = 41.0$ kg.
27) **Choice D is correct.** (5.G.4) All three angles (58°, 58°, and 64°) are less than 90 degrees, making this an acute triangle.
28) **Choice C is correct.** (5.NBT.7) $0.25 \times 4 = 1.0$ kg. Multiply: $25 \times 4 = 100$, then place decimal two places from right.
29) **Choice D is correct.** (5.G.2) The two coordinates are equal at each point. The points increase by 2 in both coordinates: (1,1), (3,3), (5,5), (7,7), (9,9).
30) **Choice A is correct.** (5.NBT.1) Converting fractions to decimals: $4 + 0.2 + 0.05 + 0.008 = 4.258$.
31) **Choice A is correct.** (5.NF.5b) $1\frac{3}{5} = \frac{8}{5}$ and $2\frac{1}{2} = \frac{5}{2}$. Multiply: $\frac{8}{5} \times \frac{5}{2} = \frac{40}{10} = 4$.
32) **Choice D is correct.** (5.NF.2) The number line shows the dot positioned at $\frac{2}{3}$. Multiplying the numerator and denominator by 2 gives $\frac{2}{3} = \frac{4}{6}$.
33) **The correct answer is 80.** (5.MD.1) $5 \times 16 = 80$ oz. Each pound has 16 ounces, so 5 pounds has five groups of 16 ounces.
34) **Choice C is correct.** (5.MD.1) Choose the operation from the story, then keep the unit with the answer. Multiply: $8 \times 45 = 360$ seeds. This confirms the answer.
35) **Choice B is correct.** (5.OA.3) The amount added grows by 1 each time: add 2, then 3, then 4, then 5. Next add 6 to get 21, then add 7 to get 28.
36) **Choice C is correct.** (5.NF.5b) Since $\frac{1}{4} < \frac{1}{2}$, the product $10 \times \frac{1}{4}$ is smaller. $10 \times \frac{1}{4} = 2\frac{1}{2}$ and $10 \times \frac{1}{2} = 5$.
37) **Choice D is correct.** (5.NF.7b) $12 \div \frac{1}{2} = 12 \times 2 = 24$.
38) **Choice D is correct.** (5.NF.7b) The x-coordinate represents units right from the origin: 9 units. The y-coordinate represents units up: 4 units. So the coordinates are $(9, 4)$.
39) **Choice A is correct.** (5.NF.2) Together eaten: $\frac{3}{8} + \frac{2}{8} = \frac{5}{8}$. Remaining: $1 - \frac{5}{8} = \frac{3}{8}$.
40) **Choice D is correct.** (5.NF.1) LCM(8,6) = 24. $\frac{5}{8} = \frac{15}{24}$ and $\frac{1}{6} = \frac{4}{24}$. $\frac{15}{24} + \frac{4}{24} = \frac{19}{24}$.

Practice Test 4 Answers and Explanations

1) **Choice C is correct.** (5.MD.3a) A rectangular prism is a 3D solid figure, so it has volume. A line segment, rectangle, and point are not solid figures with interior space.
2) **Choice C is correct.** (5.OA.2) The distributive property says multiplying the whole sum by 7 is the same as multiplying each addend by 7 and adding the products.
3) **Choice D is correct.** (5.G.4) A rectangle is a quadrilateral, and its opposite sides are parallel.

4) **Choice A is correct.** 5.G.3 A pentagon is a polygon with 5 straight sides and 5 vertices. A quadrilateral has 4 sides, and a rectangle is a type of quadrilateral.
5) **Choice B is correct.** 5.OA.1 Work from the inside out. First $12 \div 4 = 3$, then the bracket becomes $5 + 3 = 8$, and finally $8 \times 2 = 16$.
6) **Choice D is correct.** 5.OA.1 Each time we divide by a larger power of 10, the answer becomes smaller. Moving three decimal places left: $3,500 \div 1,000 = 3.5$.
7) **Choice B is correct.** 5.NBT.2 To change 2.5 to 250, move the decimal two places right. That is multiplying by 100.
8) **Choice C is correct.** 5.NF.6 One fourth of 3 yards is $\frac{1}{4} \times 3 = \frac{3}{4}$ yard.
9) **Choice C is correct.** 5.MD.4 Prism A: $4 \times 3 \times 2 = 24$ cubes. Prism B: $4 \times 3 \times 5 = 60$ cubes. Difference: $60 - 24 = 36$ unit cubes.
10) **Choice D is correct.** 5.NF.4b Ribbon per project $= \frac{3}{8} \times \frac{2}{3} = \frac{6}{24} = \frac{1}{4}$ meter.
11) **Choice D is correct.** 5.NF.2 $\frac{7}{8} - \frac{3}{8} = \frac{4}{8} = \frac{1}{2}$ of the tank.
12) **Choice A is correct.** 5.NF.5b $\frac{1}{4} \times \frac{2}{3} = \frac{2}{12}$. In the grid, 1 of the 4 rows overlaps with 2 of the 3 columns, so $1 \times 2 = 2$ cells are shaded.
13) **The correct answer is 8.2.** 5.NBT.2 Move the decimal point two places right: $0.082 \to 8.2$.
14) **Choice A is correct.** 5.NBT.2 Convert to fourths: $1\frac{2}{4} + 2\frac{1}{4} + \frac{3}{4} = 3\frac{6}{4} = 4\frac{1}{2}$ lbs.
15) **Choice B is correct.** 5.OA.2 Carol is comparing copies of the same amount, $(250 + 75)$. Two copies are more than one copy, but less than three copies.
16) **Choice A is correct.** 5.NBT.7 Line up decimal points and subtract place by place. $72.45 - 58.13 = 14.32$ degrees Fahrenheit. This confirms the answer.
17) **Choice D is correct.** 5.G.1 The origin is the point where the x-axis and y-axis intersect, labeled as $(0, 0)$.
18) **Choice B is correct.** 5.MD.1 Since 1 quart = 4 cups, divide 2 by 4: $2 \div 4 = \frac{1}{2}$ quart.
19) **Choice D is correct.** 5.NBT.4 The tenths digit is 7. Since $7 \geq 5$, round ones up: $18 \to 19$. So 18.75 seconds rounds to 19 seconds.
20) **Choice C is correct.** 5.NF.7c A sixth-box kit means 6 kits per full box. $15 \div \frac{1}{6} = 15 \times 6 = 90$ kits.
21) **The correct answer is** $(6 \times 10) \div 2$. 5.OA.2 The result of 6×10 is divided by 2, so write $(6 \times 10) \div 2$. Equivalent expressions that preserve this order are also acceptable.
22) **Choices A, B are correct.** 5.MD.5 Since the height is 5 inches, the length-times-width part must be $60 \div 5 = 12$ square inches. A gives $4 \times 3 = 12$, and B gives $6 \times 2 = 12$; C and D are too large.
23) **Choice C is correct.** 5.NBT.2 Dividing by $10^3 = 1000$ shifts the decimal 3 places left.
24) **Choice C is correct.** 5.NBT.2 The product is 9 followed by the six zeros from 1,000,000, so it has 6 zeros.
25) **Choice B is correct.** 5.MD.5 Use the rectangular-prism volume formula: $6 \times 7 \times 5 = 210$. So the volume is 210 cubic inches.
26) **The correct answer is about 1.** 5.NF.2 $\frac{1}{10} \approx 0$ and $\frac{5}{6} \approx 1$, so the benchmark estimate is about 1. For scoring, accept 1, about 1, 0.9, $\frac{9}{10}$, or the exact sum $\frac{14}{15}$.
27) **Choice A is correct.** 5.NF.2 When dividing by 100, move the decimal point 2 places to the left: $83.5 \to 8.35 \to 0.835$. So $83.5 \div 100 = 0.835$.
28) **The correct answer is 7.** 5.MD.2 Each X represents one measurement. Add the X's at each value: $2 + 4 + 1 = 7$ measurements total.
29) **Choice C is correct.** 5.MD.2 The unit fraction is the amount being shared, so divide $\frac{1}{3}$ by 4. The equation is $\frac{1}{3} \div 4 = n$.
30) **Choice D is correct.** 5.MD.5a Product of two dimensions: $12 \times 7 = 84$ cm^2. Third dimension: $336 \div 84 = 4$ cm.
31) **The correct answer is $33\frac{3}{4}$ in.** 5.MD.2 $2(5\frac{1}{4}) + 1(5\frac{1}{2}) + 3(5\frac{3}{4}) = 10\frac{1}{2} + 5\frac{1}{2} + 17\frac{1}{4} = 33\frac{3}{4}$ in.
32) **Choice B is correct.** 5.NBT.7 Round to nearest whole: $3.92 \approx 4$ and $4.18 \approx 4$. So $4 + 4 = 8$.
33) **Choice A is correct.** 5.NBT.7 Multiples of 5: 5, 10, 15, 20, ... Multiples of 4: 4, 8, 12, 16, 20, ... The least common denominator is 20.
34) **Choice A is correct.** 5.MD.1 Convert 3 kg to grams: $3 \times 1000 = 3000$ g. Add: $3000 + 250 = 3250$ g.
35) **Choice A is correct.** 5.NF.1 $10 - 6 = 4$ and $\frac{8}{10} - \frac{4}{10} = \frac{4}{10} = \frac{2}{5}$. Simplified: $4\frac{2}{5}$.
36) **Choice D is correct.** 5.NBT.2 $23 \times 10 = 230$, then $230 \times 10 = 2300$. Or $23 \times 10^2 = 2300$.
37) **Choice B is correct.** 5.NBT.2 Rule X gives $2 \times 3 = 6$. Rule Y gives $2 \times 3 + 1 = 7$.
38) **Choice B is correct.** 5.NF.7c Each whole contains 4 pieces of size $\frac{1}{4}$. With 4 wholes, there are $4 \times 4 = 16$ pieces.

39) **Choice C is correct.** 5.NBT.3b Comparing thousandths: 0.37 (370 thousandths) $<$ 0.375 (375 thousandths). The others are $\geq$ 0.375.

40) **Choice D is correct.** 5.NF.4 The number line counts four equal hops of $\frac{1}{4}$. After four fourths, you land on $\frac{4}{4} = 1$.

Practice Test 5 Answers and Explanations

1) **Choice C is correct.** 5.OA.2 Both expressions split the same total, $30 + 20$, into 5 equal parts. Dividing the sum at once or dividing each addend by 5 and then adding gives the same value.

2) **Choice C is correct.** 5.MD.5 $495 = 9 \times 5 \times 11$; $495 = 99 \times 5$. The missing dimension is 5 m.

3) **Choice A is correct.** 5.G.4 Two equal sides make the triangle isosceles. One right angle makes it a right triangle, so the name is right isosceles triangle.

4) **Choice D is correct.** 5.G.4 Looking up the table, only the Square row has check marks in BOTH "All sides equal" and "90° angles". A quadrilateral, parallelogram, and rectangle don't all guarantee equal sides; only the square does. So the most specific name is Square.

5) **The correct answer is 0.07.** 5.NBT.1 The digit 7 is in the hundredths place, so it represents $7 \times 0.01 = 0.07$.

6) **Choice B is correct.** 5.NBT.1 The second coordinate is 4 times the first. For first coordinate 5, $4 \times 5 = 20$.

7) **Choice C is correct.** 5.NF.2 The denominator increased from 9 to 27 (multiply by 3). Multiply the numerator by 3: $4 \times 3 = 12$.

8) **The correct answer is 20.** 5.G.2 Compare the y-values: $70 - 50 = 20$. The temperature changed by 20 degrees.

9) **Choice B is correct.** 5.G.2 Pattern Q is always 3 times Pattern P: $2 \times 3 = 6$, $4 \times 3 = 12$, $6 \times 3 = 18$.

10) **Choice B is correct.** 5.OA.1 First find how many pencils Ellie packed altogether: $4 \times 12 = 48$. Then subtract the 8 she gave away, so the matching expression is $(4 \times 12) - 8$.

11) **Choice C is correct.** 5.NF.2 Use ninths: $\frac{2}{3} = \frac{6}{9}$. Then $\frac{7}{9} - \frac{6}{9} = \frac{1}{9}$.

12) **Choice C is correct.** 5.NBT.5 Multiply: $156 \times 6 = (100 \times 6) + (50 \times 6) + (6 \times 6) = 600 + 300 + 36 = 936$.

13) **Choice C is correct.** 5.MD.5 Choose the operation from the story, then keep the unit with the answer. Multiply: $1,200 \times 15 = 18,000$ toys. This confirms the answer.

14) **Choice B is correct.** 5.NF.5b Since $\frac{2}{3} < 1$, the product must be less than 9. Evan's answer of 18 is double 9, which is unreasonable. The correct answer is 6.

15) **Choice A is correct.** 5.NF.7a $\frac{1}{2} \div 4 = \frac{1}{2} \times \frac{1}{4} = \frac{1}{8}$.

16) **Choice D is correct.** 5.G.2 The y-coordinate stays at 4. The x-coordinate changes from 3 to 7, which is $7 - 3 = 4$ units to the right.

17) **The correct answer is 12.009.** 5.NBT.3a Twelve wholes, then 9 thousandths means a 9 in the thousandths place: 12.009.

18) **Choice B is correct.** 5.NBT.3a $2,904 \div 44 = 66$ crates. Check: $44 \times 66 = 2,904$.

19) **Choice C is correct.** 5.NBT.7 $6.3 \div 3 = 2.1$. Think of $63 \div 3 = 21$, then place decimal one place from right: 2.1.

20) **Choice D is correct.** 5.NBT.7 $V = 12 \times 6 \times 2 = 72 \times 2 = 144$ cm^3.

21) **Choices A, B are correct.** 5.NF.1 A is true because 20 is a common denominator. B is true because $\frac{8}{20} + \frac{5}{20} = \frac{13}{20}$. C and D just add numerators/denominators.

22) **Choice D is correct.** 5.OA.3 Each term is multiplied by 10: $2,000 \times 10 = 20,000$.

23) **Choice B is correct.** 5.NF.5b $36 \times \frac{2}{9} = \frac{72}{9} = 8$ crayons. The fraction is less than 1, so the product is smaller than the original amount.

24) **Choice D is correct.** 5.MD.5c Find each part first: Prism A is $7 \times 4 \times 6 = 168$ cubic inches, and Prism B is $6 \times 4 \times 2 = 48$ cubic inches. Because the parts do not overlap, add them: $168 + 48 = 216$ cubic inches.

25) **Choice B is correct.** 5.MD.5a The room is exactly filled, so compare volumes. Room volume: $18 \times 12 \times 10 = 2160$ cubic feet. Number of boxes: $2160 \div 360 = 6$ boxes.

26) **Choice D is correct.** 5.NF.5b $2\frac{1}{4} \times 4 = \frac{9}{4} \times 4 = 9$ pounds.

27) **The correct answer is 18.** 5.NF.7b Each whole has 3 one-third pieces. Six wholes have $6 \times 3 = 18$ one-third pieces, so the quotient is 18.

28) **Choice D is correct.** 5.NF.7b Both expressions use the same base amount, $(55 + 17)$. The first expression has 6 copies of that amount, while the second has 1 copy, so the first is greater.

29) **Choice B is correct.** 5.NF.2 $\frac{4}{9}$ is close to $\frac{1}{2}$, and $\frac{1}{12}$ is small. The sum is just a little more than $\frac{1}{2}$, so $\frac{1}{2}$ is the best benchmark estimate.

30) **The correct answer is 2400.** (5.MD.1) Each kilogram has 1,000 grams. Two kilograms is 2,000 grams, and $2{,}000 + 400 = 2{,}400$ grams.
31) **Choice D is correct.** (5.MD.1) Add the board lengths: $1 + 2(1\frac{1}{4}) + 2(1\frac{1}{2}) + 1\frac{3}{4} + 2 = 9\frac{1}{4}$ feet.
32) **Choice A is correct.** (5.OA.2) The product part is 2×6. Since 5 is added to that product, the phrase is "five more than the product of 2 and 6."
33) **Choice C is correct.** (5.G.4) A rhombus has four equal sides. If it is not a square, it does not have four right angles.
34) **Choice B is correct.** (5.NF.4b) The blue region is 1 out of 5. The red region is 3 out of 4. The overlap is 3 out of 20 squares: $\frac{1}{5} \times \frac{3}{4} = \frac{3}{20}$.
35) **Choice B is correct.** (5.G.3) An isosceles triangle has 2 equal (congruent) sides. A right triangle has one 90° angle.
36) **Choice C is correct.** (5.NF.7c) Each yard has 6 one-sixth-yard pieces. $5 \div \frac{1}{6} = 5 \times 6 = 30$ cushions.
37) **Choice D is correct.** (5.NBT.2) Dividing by 1,000 moves the decimal point three places to the left. $9,200 \div 1,000 = 9.2$.
38) **Choice C is correct.** (5.NBT.2) Convert requirement to mm: 8,500 mm. Check: A = 8,400 mm (no), B = 8,700 mm (yes), C = 8,200 mm (no), D = 820,000 mm (yes). Only B and D meet it.
39) **Choice D is correct.** (5.NBT.2) Multiplying by 100 moves the decimal point 2 places to the right: $0.45 \times 100 = 45$.
40) **Choice D is correct.** (5.NBT.2) $\frac{4}{10} = \frac{2}{5}$. Then $\frac{2}{5} \times \frac{5}{8} = \frac{10}{40} = \frac{1}{4}$.

Practice Test 6 Answers and Explanations

1) **Choice B is correct.** (5.G.2) The output starts at 1 for input 1, then doubles each time. That gives outputs 1, 2, 4, 8, paired with inputs 1 through 4.
2) **Choice D is correct.** (5.NBT.7) Add: $1.45 + 2.38 = 3.83$ m (hundredths: $5 + 8 = 13$, regroup; tenths: $4 + 3 + 1 = 8$; ones: $1 + 2 = 3$).
3) **Choice D is correct.** (5.NF.6) $\frac{2}{3} \times 1\frac{1}{2} = \frac{2}{3} \times \frac{3}{2} = \frac{6}{6} = 1$ cup.
4) **Choice C is correct.** (5.NBT.2) The table shows $29.7 \div 10 = 2.97$. Move decimal 1 place left.
5) **Choice D is correct.** (5.NBT.3a) In the decimal 2.34, the 3 is in the tenths place (0.3) and the 4 is in the hundredths place (0.04). So $2.34 = 2 + 0.3 + 0.04$.
6) **Choice C is correct.** (5.NBT.2) Multiplying by 100 moves the decimal two places right: $0.7 \to 7 \to 70$.
7) **The correct answer is 42.** (5.MD.4) A 7 by 2 layer has 14 cubes. With 3 layers, $14 \times 3 = 42$ cubic units.
8) **The correct answer is 21.** (5.MD.4) First simplify the parentheses: $6 + 2 = 8$. Then $48 \div 8 = 6$ and $5 \times 3 = 15$, so the total is $6 + 15 = 21$.
9) **Choice D is correct.** (5.OA.1) Line up decimal points and subtract place by place. $12.50 - 8.75 = 3.75$ miles. This confirms the answer.
10) **Choice B is correct.** (5.NBT.3b) Point B is at 0.525, which is 0.025 from 0.5. Point A (0.205) is 0.295 away, and C (0.75) is 0.25 away. Point B is closest.
11) **Choice A is correct.** (5.NF.7b) A whole divided into 5 equal parts of $\frac{1}{5}$ each is represented by $1 \div \frac{1}{5} = 5$.
12) **The correct answer is 5.** (5.MD.5) The base area is $8 \times 5 = 40$ square meters. Since $200 \div 40 = 5$, the height is 5 m.
13) **Choice B is correct.** (5.MD.5) $7\frac{1}{2} - 3\frac{1}{2} = (7 - 3) + (\frac{1}{2} - \frac{1}{2}) = 4 + 0 = 4$ m.
14) **Choice B is correct.** (5.G.2) The x-coordinate (40) is units sold, and the y-coordinate (200) is revenue in dollars. So 40 units were sold for $200.
15) **Choice C is correct.** (5.NF.2) $\frac{5}{6} = \frac{5\times4}{6\times4} = \frac{20}{24}$ and $\frac{3}{8} = \frac{3\times3}{8\times3} = \frac{9}{24}$.
16) **Choice C is correct.** (5.NBT.2) Both equal 5000: $50 \times 100 = 5000$ and $500 \times 10 = 5000$.
17) **Choice B is correct.** (5.NF.1) Add whole: $1 + 3 = 4$. Add fractions: $\frac{2}{5} + \frac{1}{5} = \frac{3}{5}$. Result: $4\frac{3}{5}$.
18) **Choices A, B are correct.** (5.NBT.6) $13 \times 65 = 845$ exactly, so the quotient is 65 with no remainder. C and D miscalculate.
19) **Choice C is correct.** (5.MD.1) Number of sections: $72 \div 8 = 9$. Posts needed: $9 + 1 = 10$ (one at each end and one at each division between sections).
20) **Choice C is correct.** (5.NF.7c) Each whole contains 2 pieces of size $\frac{1}{2}$. With 1 whole, there are $1 \times 2 = 2$ pieces.
21) **Choice A is correct.** (5.G.1) Both J at (2, 4) and K at (7, 4) have y-coordinate 4, so they share the same y-coordinate.
22) **Choice B is correct.** (5.NF.1) LCM(9,3) = 9. $\frac{1}{3} = \frac{3}{9}$. $\frac{4}{9} + \frac{3}{9} = \frac{7}{9}$.

23) **Choice D is correct.** (5.NF.1) The tenths digit is 3. The hundredths digit is 4. Since $4 < 5$, keep tenths as 3: 11.348 $\rightarrow$ 11.3. Maya is correct.

24) **Choice A is correct.** (5.MD.1) 1 yard = 3 feet. So 2 yards = $2 \times 3 = 6$ feet. The bar model shows 3 feet per yard for 2 yards.

25) **Choice D is correct.** (5.NF.7c) The model asks how many one-third pieces fit in 5 wholes. So the matching equation is $5 \div \frac{1}{3} = n$.

26) **Choice C is correct.** (5.NBT.2) The nonzero parts make $2 \times 5 = 10$, which contributes one trailing zero. The factors already have four zeros, so the product has 5 zeros.

27) **Choice D is correct.** (5.NF.4) $\frac{7}{8} \times 2 = \frac{14}{8} = 1\frac{6}{8} = 1\frac{3}{4}$ (simplified).

28) **Choice A is correct.** (5.NF.2) Removed: $\frac{1}{5} + \frac{2}{7} = \frac{7}{35} + \frac{10}{35} = \frac{17}{35}$. Remaining: $1 - \frac{17}{35} = \frac{18}{35}$ cup.

29) **Choice C is correct.** (5.NBT.1) A digit in the tenths place ($0.6 = \frac{6}{10}$) is 10 times greater than the same digit in the hundredths place ($0.06 = \frac{6}{100}$).

30) **Choice C is correct.** (5.MD.5) Use the rectangular-prism volume formula: $6 \times 7 \times 8 = 336$. So the volume is 336 cubic feet.

31) **Choice C is correct.** (5.MD.2) Count the X marks at each height on the line plot. The height with the greatest number of X marks is 5 inches, which has 4 plants. Therefore, the most common plant height is 5 inches.

32) **Choice C is correct.** (5.MD.3a) $5 \times 4 \times 3 = 60$ unit cubes. Volume is the product of length, width, and height.

33) **The correct answer is 0.24.** (5.NBT.7) $4 \times 6 = 24$. Two decimal places total in factors, so 0.24.

34) **Choice B is correct.** (5.NBT.7) Check each product carefully. A: $4 \times 3 \times 6 = 72$. B: $6 \times 2 \times 7 = 84$. C: $5 \times 3 \times 6 = 90$. D: $4 \times 5 \times 4 = 80$. Only the second prism has volume 84 cm^3.

35) **Choice D is correct.** (5.NF.5b) Convert to improper fractions: $4\frac{1}{3} = \frac{13}{3}$ and $1\frac{1}{2} = \frac{3}{2}$. Then $\frac{13}{3} \times \frac{3}{2} = \frac{13}{2} = 6\frac{1}{2}$.

36) **Choice A is correct.** (5.OA.3) Check the rows: $1 \times 3 - 1 = 2$, $2 \times 3 - 1 = 5$, and $3 \times 3 - 1 = 8$. The same rule works for the table.

37) **Choice C is correct.** (5.G.2) Following the pattern: point 1 is (1, 2), point 2 is (3, 5), point 3 is (5, 8), point 4 is (7, 11).

38) **The correct answer is 700.** (5.NBT.2) $10^2 = 100$, so $7 \times 10^2 = 7 \times 100 = 700$.

39) **Choice A is correct.** (5.NBT.2) Dividing each term in Sequence 1 by 5 gives Sequence 2: 5÷5=1, 10÷5=2, 15÷5=3, etc.

40) **Choice B is correct.** (5.G.4) Figure B is described as having exactly one pair of parallel sides, so it is not a parallelogram. Figures A and D are in the parallelogram family because they have two pairs of parallel sides.

Practice Test 7 Answers and Explanations

1) **Choice A is correct.** (5.NBT.2) $600 \div 100 = 6$. (B gives 60; C gives 0.6; D gives 0.06).

2) **Choice C is correct.** (5.NBT.2) The four points form a quadrilateral with four right angles and opposite sides equal. This is a rectangle with width 6 units and height 4 units.

3) **Choice B is correct.** (5.MD.5c) Find each part first: Prism A is $5 \times 4 \times 6 = 120$ cubic inches, and Prism B is $6 \times 4 \times 2 = 48$ cubic inches. Because the parts do not overlap, add them: $120 + 48 = 168$ cubic inches.

4) **Choice D is correct.** (5.NBT.5) Multiply: $39 \times 28 = 39 \times (30 - 2) = (39 \times 30) - (39 \times 2) = 1,170 - 78 = 1,092$ seats.

5) **Choice C is correct.** (5.NF.2) $\frac{4}{8} = \frac{4 \div 4}{8 \div 4} = \frac{1}{2}$. In simplest form, this is one half of the inventory.

6) **Choice C is correct.** (5.G.4) All three sides have tick marks (equal), and all angles are 60 degrees (acute), making it equilateral acute.

7) **Choice D is correct.** (5.NF.5b) $8 \times \frac{3}{8} = 3$ slices. The scaling factor $\frac{3}{8}$ is less than 1, so the result is smaller than 8.

8) **Choice D is correct.** (5.NF.2) LCD = 12. $\frac{3}{4} = \frac{9}{12}$; $\frac{1}{3} = \frac{4}{12}$. $\frac{9}{12} - \frac{4}{12} = \frac{5}{12}$.

9) **Choice A is correct.** (5.OA.2) The first expression makes 3 copies of $20 - 5$. The second expression subtracts 3 copies of 5 from only one 20. The first expression is greater.

10) **Choice C is correct.** (5.OA.1) Parentheses come first: $4 + 5 = 9$. Then $36 \div 9 = 4$, and $4 + 6 = 10$.

11) **Choice A is correct.** (5.OA.1) Figures with 4 equal sides include the rhombuses that are not squares and the squares: $4 + 3 = 7$.

12) **The correct answer is 360 ft^3.** (5.MD.5a) $15 \times 4 \times 6 = 360$ ft^3.

13) **Choice B is correct.** (5.MD.5a) $6+2\times 3-1=6+6-1=11$ (not 16). Adding $(6+2)$ changes order of ops. (2×3) doesn't change result.
14) **Choice B is correct.** (5.MD.4) If there are 2 layers with 6 cubes each: $6+6=12$ or $6\times 2=12$ unit cubes.
15) **Choice B is correct.** (5.MD.2) The plot shows $41\frac{1}{2}$ ounces of juice in all: $(4\times 2)+(4\frac{1}{2}\times 4)+(5\times 2)+(5\frac{1}{2}\times 1)=41\frac{1}{2}$. Each serving is $\frac{1}{2}$ ounce, so $41\frac{1}{2}\div\frac{1}{2}=83$ servings.
16) **Choice A is correct.** (5.MD.5) The base area is $14\times 7=98$ square centimeters. Since $392\div 98=4$, the height is 4 cm.
17) **The correct answer is 30.** (5.OA.1) Left: $3+3=6$, $36\div 6=6$. Right: $2\times 3=6$, $6\times 4=24$. Sum: $6+24=30$.
18) **The correct answer is 6 ft.** (5.OA.1) The base area is $7\times 5=35$ square feet. Since $210\div 35=6$, the height is 6 ft.
19) **Choices A, B are correct.** (5.MD.5a) Two notebooks cost $2\times 3.25=6.50$, so A is true. One notebook and two pens cost $3.25+2\times 1.15=5.55$, so B is true. C and D miscompute.
20) **Choice C is correct.** (5.NF.2) $4\frac{2}{3}\approx 5$ and $5\frac{1}{4}\approx 5$. So $4\frac{2}{3}+5\frac{1}{4}\approx 5+5=10$.
21) **Choice C is correct.** (5.NBT.2) A power of 10 tells how many factors of 10 to use. 10^2 means $10\times 10=100$. This confirms the answer.
22) **Choice B is correct.** (5.NBT.2) Add hundredths and tenths carefully: $3.87+4.92=8.79$.
23) **Choice B is correct.** (5.NBT.7) Both expressions multiply 24 by a fraction. Since $\frac{4}{5}>\frac{2}{3}$, $\frac{4}{5}\times 24$ has the larger value.
24) **Choice D is correct.** (5.MD.1) Total bags: $12+8=20$ bags. Weight: $20\times 25=500$ pounds. Since 500 is one fourth of 2,000, the total weight is $\frac{1}{4}$ ton.
25) **Choice B is correct.** (5.NF.1) LCM(2,3,6) = 6. $\frac{1}{2}=\frac{3}{6}$, $\frac{1}{3}=\frac{2}{6}$, $\frac{1}{6}=\frac{1}{6}$. $\frac{3}{6}+\frac{2}{6}+\frac{1}{6}=\frac{6}{6}=1$.
26) **Choice A is correct.** (5.NF.4) For 3 pans, use 3 copies of $\frac{1}{3}$ cup. $3\times\frac{1}{3}=\frac{3}{3}=1$, so the recipe needs 1 cup of sugar.
27) **Choice A is correct.** (5.NBT.7) $11.25-5.43=5.82$. Align decimals and subtract each place.
28) **Choice C is correct.** (5.NBT.7) Each pound has 16 ounces. $45\times 16=720$, so 45 pounds equals 720 ounces.
29) **Choice C is correct.** (5.NBT.6) $2,145\div 65=33$ cupcakes per order. Check: $65\times 33=2,145$.
30) **Choice C is correct.** (5.MD.1) 1 centimeter = 10 millimeters. Multiply: $24\times 10=240$ mm.
31) **Choice A is correct.** (5.MD.3a) $1\times 8\times 4=32$ cu. units. Choice B: $1\times 4\times 7=28$. Choice C: $3\times 4\times 3=36$. Choice D: $2\times 3\times 5=30$.
32) **Choice C is correct.** (5.G.1) For $(2,6)$: x-coordinate 2 means 2 units right; y-coordinate 6 means 6 units up.
33) **The correct answer is $\frac{1}{8}$.** (5.NF.7a) $\frac{1}{4}\div 2=\frac{1}{4}\times\frac{1}{2}=\frac{1}{8}$.
34) **Choice C is correct.** (5.NF.7a) $6\div\frac{1}{4}=6\times 4=24$. There are 24 portions.
35) **Choice C is correct.** (5.NBT.2) Multiplying by 1,000 moves the decimal three places right: $0.04\to 0.4\to 4\to 40$.
36) **Choice A is correct.** (5.NBT.2) Each whole contains 3 pieces of size $\frac{1}{3}$. With 5 wholes, there are $5\times 3=15$ pieces.
37) **Choice D is correct.** (5.NBT.3b) Both represent 2 ones and 5 tenths. Trailing zeros are equivalent.
38) **Choice D is correct.** (5.G.2) For input 4, $4\times 4-2=14$, not 15. The correct pair would be $(4,14)$.
39) **Choice B is correct.** (5.NBT.4) 8.29 has tenths=2 and hundredths=9. Since $9\geq 5$, round tenths up: $2\to 3$, giving 8.3. The other choices round to 8.2 or 8.4.
40) **Choice D is correct.** (5.MD.5) Use the rectangular-prism volume formula: $5\times 5\times 3=75$. So the volume is 75 cubic meters.

Practice Test 8 Answers and Explanations

1) **Choice A is correct.** (5.NF.1) Write $10=9\frac{7}{7}$. Then $9\frac{7}{7}-3\frac{2}{7}=6\frac{5}{7}$.
2) **The correct answer is 5.** (5.G.2) The first number in an ordered pair is the x-coordinate.
3) **Choice C is correct.** (5.G.2) Choose the operation from the story, then keep the unit with the answer. Subtract: $250-165.5=84.5$ liters needed. This confirms the answer.
4) **Choice C is correct.** (5.NBT.2) The pattern adds one zero each time the multiplier grows by a factor of 10. With 1,000, the product is 15,000.
5) **Choice D is correct.** (5.NBT.2) $27\times 100=2700$. Append two zeros to 27.
6) **Choice C is correct.** (5.NBT.2) Convert to fourths: $2\frac{2}{4}+1\frac{3}{4}=3\frac{5}{4}=4\frac{1}{4}$ m.

7) **Choice D is correct.** (5.NF.2) Multiples of 7 are found by multiplying 7 by 1, 2, 3, 4: $7 \times 1 = 7$, $7 \times 2 = 14$, $7 \times 3 = 21$, $7 \times 4 = 28$.

8) **Choice C is correct.** (5.MD.5a) $V = l \times w \times h = 3 \times 2 \times 5 = 30$ in^3.

9) **The correct answer is 2.** (5.G.2) For each point, $2 \div 1 = 2$, $4 \div 2 = 2$, and $6 \div 3 = 2$.

10) **Choice B is correct.** (5.G.2) One fifth of an amount means split it into 5 equal parts. So one fifth of $(100 - 25)$ is $(100 - 25) \div 5$.

11) **The correct answer is $\frac{5}{9}$.** (5.NF.5b) Multiplying by 1 does not change the value, so $1 \times \frac{5}{9} = \frac{5}{9}$.

12) **Choice D is correct.** (5.NF.5b) $\frac{3}{8} + \frac{1}{8} = \frac{4}{8} = \frac{1}{2}$ of the land is planted.

13) **Choice A is correct.** (5.NBT.1) In 2.894, the digits after the decimal are: 8 (tenths), 9 (hundredths), 4 (thousandths). The student mistook 4 for being in the tenths place.

14) **Choice C is correct.** (5.OA.1) Evaluate each expression. A equals 20, B equals 18, C equals $2 \times 6 = 12$, and D equals 15.

15) **Choice D is correct.** (5.NBT.2) $4.2 \div 100 = 0.042$. A equals 4.2, while C and D each equal 0.42. B matches.

16) **Choice D is correct.** (5.NBT.2) The base area is $10 \times 9 = 90$ square inches. Since $360 \div 90 = 4$, the height is 4 inches.

17) **Choice B is correct.** (5.NF.6) First part: $\frac{3}{4} \times 16 = 12$ miles. Remaining: $16 - 12 = 4$ miles. Second part: $\frac{1}{2} \times 4 = 2$ miles. Total: $12 + 2 = 14$ miles.

18) **Choice A is correct.** (5.NBT.2) $0.032 \times 100 = 3.2$ (move decimal 2 places right). The statement is true.

19) **Choice A is correct.** (5.NF.4b) Spaghetti occupies $\frac{2}{5} \times \frac{3}{4} = \frac{6}{20}$ of total shelf space.

20) **Choice A is correct.** (5.MD.2) There are two ribbons at $\frac{1}{2}$ inch. Their total length is $\frac{1}{2} + \frac{1}{2} = 1$ inch.

21) **Choice A is correct.** (5.NF.5b) "Half of 3/4" means $\frac{1}{2} \times \frac{3}{4} = \frac{3}{8}$.

22) **Choices A, B, C are correct.** (5.MD.5c) Volume is measured in cubic units. For non-overlapping rectangular prisms, multiply each part's dimensions and add the part volumes.

23) **Choice B is correct.** (5.NBT.7) The area model breaks into four parts: $3 \times 2 = 6$, $3 \times 0.5 = 1.5$, $0.2 \times 2 = 0.4$, $0.2 \times 0.5 = 0.1$. Total: $6 + 1.5 + 0.4 + 0.1 = 8$.

24) **Choice A is correct.** (5.NF.7a) $\frac{1}{5} \div 4 = \frac{1}{5} \times \frac{1}{4} = \frac{1}{20}$.

25) **The correct answer is 5.** (5.OA.3) $5 = 5 \times 1$, $10 = 5 \times 2$, etc. Each A term is 5 times its B term.

26) **The correct answer is hexagon.** (5.G.3) A hexagon has 6 sides. Because all sides and angles are equal, regular hexagon is a more specific name, but hexagon is also correct.

27) **Choice C is correct.** (5.G.3) Only $\frac{5}{7} < 1$. The others equal 1 or exceed 1, so their products would be ≥ 28.

28) **Choice D is correct.** (5.NF.7c) $7 \div \frac{1}{4} = 7 \times 4 = 28$ pieces.

29) **Choice D is correct.** (5.NF.7c) Use total amount divided by the size of one piece. The equation is $8 \div \frac{1}{4} = n$.

30) **Choice B is correct.** (5.NBT.3a) The digit 8 is in the hundredths place (third column from the left, or second position after the decimal point).

31) **Choice D is correct.** (5.G.2) The x-coordinate represents hours studied (5 hours) and the y-coordinate represents the test score (85 points). So the point $(5, 85)$ means a student studied for 5 hours and earned a score of 85.

32) **Choice C is correct.** (5.MD.5a) Volume = base area × height = $48 \times 5 = 240$ ft^3.

33) **Choice B is correct.** (5.OA.3) Rule: Output = $7\times$ Input; $7 \times 4 = 28$.

34) **Choice A is correct.** (5.NF.2) Divide the numerator and denominator by 2: $\frac{2}{10} = \frac{1}{5}$.

35) **Choice A is correct.** (5.NF.5b) $\frac{1}{3} \times 3\frac{1}{3} = \frac{1}{3} \times \frac{10}{3} = \frac{10}{9} = 1\frac{1}{9}$ cups.

36) **Choice D is correct.** (5.G.4) An isosceles triangle has at least two equal sides, which also means it has two equal angles. This triangle has three different angle measures, so it is right scalene, not isosceles.

37) **Choice B is correct.** (5.NBT.5) Multiply: $23 \times 11 = 23 \times (10 + 1) = (23 \times 10) + (23 \times 1) = 230 + 23 = 253$.

38) **Choice C is correct.** (5.NF.2) $\frac{1}{4} = \frac{3}{12}$. $\frac{11}{12} - \frac{3}{12} = \frac{8}{12} = \frac{2}{3}$.

39) **Choice A is correct.** (5.G.4) A quadrilateral is any four-sided polygon. Since every parallelogram has four sides, every parallelogram is also a quadrilateral.

40) **Choice A is correct.** (5.OA.2) In $4 \times (15 + 7)$, the 4 is multiplied by both 15 and 7. In $4 \times 15 + 7$, only 15 is multiplied by 4, with one 7 added afterward. The first expression is greater.

Testinar Grade 5 Online Center

So Much More Online! *Discover amazing resources to help you succeed!*

Testinar Math Grade 5 Online Center offers a complete study program, including:

- ✓ **All the tools you need to master Grade 5 math concepts**
- ✓ **Printable practice sets that sharpen daily problem-solving**
- ✓ **Free full-length Grade 5 math practice tests to track progress**
- ✓ **Study guides and pacing tips that fit real classroom schedules**
- ✓ **And much more ...**

Scan Me

No Registration Required! Start learning right away—it's completely free and easy! **Visit Testinar.com/Grade5** *You've got this! Keep learning and growing!*

First Mate, Well Done!

◇ You sailed through 8 practice tests with steady hands and a sharp eye. The waters got rough sometimes, but you kept your course. That's what good sailors do. Now the harbor (test day) is in sight, and you are ready to dock with confidence. ◇

⋆ **Captain's wisdom:** a good sailor doesn't fight the wind—they read it and adjust. On a test, the same thing is true. When a problem feels tricky, don't panic. Read it again. Try a new strategy. Adjust the sails of your thinking. ⋆

Captain's Skills Inventory

- **Steady Steering:** EXCELLENT! You stay on course even when problems get tough.
- **Wind Reading:** STRONG! You can spot what a problem is really asking.
- **Crew Spirit:** HIGH! You believe in your own ability.
- **Harbor Approach:** READY! You know how to finish a test calmly.

Final captain's note: the best voyages combine planning with courage. You have both. Trust the chart you built through these 8 tests. Trust your hands on the wheel. Then sail confidently into test day.

If you'd like to share your experience or have questions, please email me at reza@testinar.com. I'd love to hear from you!

Reza Nazari & Jay Daie

Your Math Captain (Smooth Sailing Ahead)

www.ingramcontent.com/pod-product-compliance
Lightning Source LLC
LaVergne TN
LVHW081251100826
845148LV00009B/1194

* 9 7 9 8 9 0 5 3 4 0 0 9 3 *